THIS IS CHRISTMAS,
Song by Song

THIS IS CHRISTMAS,
Song by Song

———— ✦ ————

The Stories Behind 100 Holiday Hits

ANNIE ZALESKI

————

Illustrated by Darling Clementine

RUNNING PRESS
PHILADELPHIA

Running Press
Hachette Book Group
1290 Avenue of the Americas, New York, NY 10104
www.runningpress.com
@Running_Press

Printed in China

First Edition: October 2023

Published by Running Press, an imprint of Perseus Books, LLC, a subsidiary of Hachette Book Group, Inc. The Running Press name and logo are trademarks of the Hachette Book Group.

The Hachette Speakers Bureau provides a wide range of authors for speaking events. To find out more, go to www.hachettespeakersbureau.com or email HachetteSpeakers@hbgusa.com.

Running Press books may be purchased in bulk for business, educational, or promotional use. For more information, please contact your local bookseller or the Hachette Book Group Special Markets Department at Special.Markets@hbgusa.com.

The publisher is not responsible for websites (or their content) that are not owned by the publisher.

Print book cover and interior design by Joanna Price.

Library of Congress Control Number: 2023901305

ISBNs: 978-0-7624-8272-6 (hardcover), 978-0-7624-8273-3 (ebook)

APS

10 9 8 7 6 5 4 3 2 1

*To my parents, especially my dad—the biggest
Mannheim Steamroller and Trans-Siberian
Orchestra fan I know—and to my husband, Matt*

Contents

Introduction

___

When you think of Christmas music, what comes to mind? Chances are good it's mentions of snow, mistletoe, presents, Santa Claus, and decking the halls—or it's the soothing sound of sleigh bells or jingle bells, shaking ever so lightly in the background. Maybe holiday songs symbolize the warm, fuzzy feelings of family together time, the carefree whimsy of childhood, or the kind of cozy romance that gets your heart pumping. Perhaps it's the way Christmas tunes can provide a moment of solemn reflection—or, alternately, they might function instead as a silly, lighthearted escape from holiday stress.

In other words, Christmas songs are much more eclectic—and offer quite a bit more emotional depth—than you might initially think. Perhaps unsurprisingly, the history of Christmas music mirrors the history of popular music. Orchestras, jazz musicians, and big bands played festive tunes in the 1930s and 1940s, while the emergence of rock 'n' roll in the 1950s injected some guitar-driven pep into Christmas music's step. Once the Beatles shook up popular culture, that opened the door for holiday music across all genres—soft rock, soul, glam, punk, R&B, and synth-pop—to add pizzazz to the usual throwback Christmas classics and retro-cool standards.

Over the years, Christmas tunes have also often reflected contemporary history and culture. This can be positive—Elton John recorded 1973's "Step into Christmas" at the end of a triumphant year full of chart success—or sobering. During World War II, Bing Crosby's "White Christmas" and "I'll Be Home for Christmas" resonated with soldiers and their families navigating challenging wartime separations, while the 1984 charity single "Do They Know It's Christmas?"

raised funds to benefit people affected by famine in Ethiopia. The subtext around the clandestine smooching in "I Saw Mommy Kissing Santa Claus," meanwhile, raised some eyebrows and even led to the song being banned in a few places.

Christmas music can also ebb and flow in popularity. Sometimes that's thanks to movie placements—just ask Brenda Lee about the positive impact from "Rockin' Around the Christmas Tree" appearing in 1990's *Home Alone*—or simply changing times. Producer Phil Spector's 2009 murder conviction overshadowed his earlier work and career, including the seminal LP *A Christmas Gift for You from Phil Spector*, while "Baby, It's Cold Outside" has drawn criticism in this modern age. Other songs have become extremely polarizing for reasons that are difficult to pinpoint—like Paul McCartney's synthesizer-driven "Wonderful Christmastime."

At the end of the day, Christmas music is deeply fascinating and illuminates greater truths about us and our world. *This Is Christmas, Song by Song* delves into the stories behind the 100 most meaningful Christmas songs of all time—the weird, the surprising, the touching, the festive. Some of these songs have straightforward origin stories; others have convoluted (or even exaggerated) histories. Oddly, many of them were written during the dog days of summer, when Christmas was still months away, and not as many as you might think have religious roots or are considered traditional songs.

These 100 songs are arranged in chronological order by year of release. That's because ranking them by quality is just too difficult—and this method makes the evolution of Christmas music that much more prominent. Yet if there's one thing all 100 songs have in common, it's that they're all part of a celebratory holiday season. So grab a candy cane (or two), throw on your best Christmas music mix, and please enjoy.

TWELVE DAYS
OF CHRISTMAS

TRADITIONAL

Songwriter: Traditional; modern version by Frederic Austin
Also covered by: Bing Crosby & the Andrews Sisters, Bob &
Doug McKenzie, the Muppets and John Denver, Twisted Sister

WHAT'S BETTER THAN receiving presents from a loved one on Christmas morning? How about presents from a loved one for *12 straight days* during the Christmas season? That's the premise of the traditional song "Twelve Days of Christmas." These gifts range in scope and size—geese laying eggs, a handful of gold rings, ladies milking, drummers—although the haul always ends with a lone partridge perched in a pear tree. (Say that five times fast!)

The 12 days of Christmas are a real holiday commemorated by Christians to celebrate the birth of Jesus. However, the basic framework of the song and its giving theme originated in a 1780 children's book called *Mirth without Mischief*. Over the subsequent centuries, the words evolved and shifted as other writers interpreted and passed down the story.

At the start of the 20th century, the English composer Frederic Austin—who also restored the score for *The Beggar's*

Opera—drew on the earliest version of the words and developed a melody for them. He copyrighted the resulting song, "Twelve Days of Christmas," in 1909, after having played it live for a few years before. In a footnote of a later reprint of the song, Austin noted, "This song was, in my childhood, current in my family. I have not met with the tune of it elsewhere, nor with the particular version of the words, and have, in this setting, recorded both to the best of my recollection."

Austin's version was well-received. A 1909 review in the *Manchester Courier and Lancashire General Advertiser* described it as "effectively arranged" even if "both words and music are more curious than beautiful." That year, Austin's new composition was also performed live, including at a December concert in Leicester, England, where it was described as a "seasonal novelty in the shape of a traditional air."

The "Twelve Days of Christmas" has been redone in a humorous way, as Bob Rivers did with the "12 Pains of Christmas" (among other gifts: a hangover), and also in a straightforward manner by dozens of artists. Although in the modern world we might not welcome some of the gifts—swans aren't necessarily very practical *and* they're expensive—the generous sentiment at the song's core stands.

WHITE CHRISTMAS

1942 • BING CROSBY

Songwriter: Irving Berlin
Also covered by: Michael Bublé, Frank Sinatra, Meghan Trainor
featuring Seth MacFarlane, Andy Williams

THE HOLIDAYS ARE supposed to be cheerful and carefree, a time to break bread and be merry with loved ones. But what if there's a holiday season when joy is in short supply?

That's the scenario posed by "White Christmas," which became a hit as World War II intensified during the fall and winter of 1942. Written by Irving Berlin and performed by Bing Crosby, the song leans into holiday sadness. The narrator becomes deeply nostalgic while writing out Christmas cards, as it's strongly suggested that the good tidings in the greetings are at odds with reality. In fact, the narrator pins their hopes and dreams on the possibility of a snow-filled Christmas, as that bit of whimsy represents not just a postcard-pretty setting but also simpler days and happier times.

Berlin started sketching out the song in January 1940, bringing an early draft into his office bright and early on a Monday morning. "Not only is it the best song *I* ever wrote, it's the best song anybody ever wrote," he reportedly said to his secretary, as noted in the book *White Christmas: The Story of an American Song*. However, Berlin had been ruminating on a song called "White Christmas" for a few years. A tune by the same name, but with a less somber vibe, appeared in 1938 as part of a never-produced Berlin show called *The Crystal Ball*.

Nevertheless, Berlin finally dug in and finished the circa-1940 "White Christmas" for the 1942 movie *Holiday Inn*, which costarred Crosby and Fred Astaire. Anticipation for the film began building almost a year in advance.

Newspaper articles from 1941 touted that *Holiday Inn* had the most original music ever used in a film and teased the movie's holiday-filled musical premise.

Buzz also started gathering around "White Christmas" specifically during the 1941 holiday season. In December, right after the attack on Pearl Harbor prompted the US to enter World War II, "White Christmas" was one of several Crosby holiday songs flown to England on a bomber airplane, at the behest of the British government. On Christmas 1941, Crosby also played the song on his NBC radio show, *The Kraft Music Hall*. A scratchy recording of this broadcast on acetate disk is solemn and aching, matching the national mood at the time.

Crosby was the perfect vocalist to deliver such a reassuring message. His delivery is sonorous and deeply empathetic. It's not just aspirational listening to him croon lines about bygone perfect Christmases with pristine snow, children on their best behavior for Santa, and actual time to send handwritten cards. When the song ends, listeners truly believe they can achieve such an idyllic Christmas once again, whether very soon or in the future.

In the lead-up to the 1942 release of *Holiday Inn*, Crosby rerecorded "White Christmas" for Decca Records on May 29 at LA's Radio Recorders studio. This new version is as reassuring and welcoming as the older take. On the recording is John Scott Trotter and His Orchestra—which contributes restrained, longing-filled strings, twinkling percussion, and velvety horns—and the Ken Darby Singers. The latter is a somber, coed choir that enters the song's mix gradually. At times, they join forces with Crosby, while at other times they take the vocal lead. The net effect is that "White Christmas" makes listeners feel like they're not alone in feeling blue—in fact, there's a whole chorus of people ready to offer solace.

This version of "White Christmas" became a sensation when it was released, spending 11 weeks at No. 1 on the National Best-Selling Retail Records chart beginning the week of Halloween 1942. The song also topped charts again each year between 1945 and 1947. Crosby rerecorded the song again in 1947, faithfully re-creating the "White Christmas" magic.

The song is still listed in the *Guinness Book of World Records* as the best-selling single of all time, with a staggering 50 million copies sold, although its movie roots weren't forgotten: "White Christmas" won an Oscar for Best Original Song, and Crosby starred in a 1954 remake of *Holiday Inn*, called *White Christmas*. To this day, the single is a staple of the holiday music season, telegraphing comfort to anyone who isn't feeling festive.

I'LL BE HOME FOR CHRISTMAS

1943 • BING CROSBY

Songwriters: Kim Gannon, Walter Kent, Samuel "Buck" Ram
Also covered by: The Carpenters, Kelly Clarkson, Johnny Mathis, Elvis Presley

BING CROSBY BEGAN 1943 on top of the entertainment world. Two films in which he costarred, *Holiday Inn* and *Road to Morocco*, made the list of top-grossing films of 1942. His single "White Christmas," meanwhile, was finishing out an 11-week run atop the National Best-Selling Retail Records chart and had become an instant holiday classic.

However, in the real world, things weren't quite as rosy. World War II was raging across Europe and the Pacific and wartime anxiety and stress were running high, as families dealt with separation from loved ones, food rations, and plenty of uncertainty. Enter Crosby's 1943 contribution to the holiday canon, "I'll Be Home for Christmas," which captured the longing and sorrow of this fraught time. Simple yet effective, the song features a narrator who equates the holiday with small pleasures—snow, presents, and mistletoe—and tries to be reassuring about their chances of being home for the holidays.

If this sounds like the nostalgic scene Crosby described in "White Christmas," that's not entirely off base, as the two songs do have obvious parallels. "I'll Be Home for Christmas" also features sparkling accompaniment from John Scott Trotter and His Orchestra, while Crosby's vocal delivery here once again possesses both empathy and authority. Newspapers also naturally compared the two songs, with the *Minneapolis Star* noting, "This year's ditty has the same sentimental appeal."

However, "I'll Be Home for Christmas" is decidedly less optimistic than "White Christmas," with lyrics hinting that coming home for the holidays is sadly just a fantasy. The song's title underlines this bad news, as it's sometimes rendered with the parenthetical "If Only in My Dreams." On another version of the song, Crosby is also joined by a chorus of male and female voices as the song progresses. The nod to wartime sorrows is impossible to miss: The men sound solemn as they sing lines about being home for Christmas, while women chime in on the lyrics about promising to have snow and gifts waiting.

The original 10-inch shellac single issued on Decca Records credited the song to Walter Kent and Kim Gannon; the duo worked as an architect and lawyer, respectively, before forming a songwriting team. However, Samuel "Buck" Ram— who would later find fame as the producer of the Platters—soon also earned a songwriting credit after a bout of litigation.

According to the Library of Congress, Ram copyrighted a song called "I'll Be Home for Christmas (Tho' Just in Memory)" in 1942. *Billboard* reported at the time that Ram had apparently shared this song with Walter Kent and even discussed a potential collaboration that didn't pan out. However, when the Kent-Gannon composition "I'll Be Home for Christmas" emerged in 1943, Ram's publisher wasn't thrilled and filed a copyright infringement lawsuit. The suit was settled within weeks, *Billboard* noted; among other settlement terms, Ram was added as one of the songwriters.

Despite the controversy, "I'll Be Home for Christmas" ended up becoming a holiday favorite in 1943, peaking at No. 3 on *Billboard*'s National Best-Selling Retail Records chart. The song was covered countless times in the subsequent decades, as its sorrowful tone resonated with anyone who was missing relatives during the Christmas season. In a sign of its universal nature, "I'll Be Home for Christmas" also eventually grew to become a touchstone for all kinds of homecomings. Most notably, in December 1965, when astronauts Frank Borman and James Lovell were winding down a then-record 330 hours in space on Gemini 7, the song was chosen to usher them back to Earth.

HAVE YOURSELF A MERRY LITTLE CHRISTMAS

1944 • JUDY GARLAND

Songwriters: Ralph Blane and Hugh Martin
Also covered by: Christina Aguilera, Tori Amos, Michael Bublé, Frank Sinatra

JUDY GARLAND STARTED dabbling in more grown-up musical fare after her star-making role in *The Wizard of Oz*. In the 1944 MGM film *Meet Me in St. Louis*, which details the whirlwind lives of the Smith family of St. Louis, she portrays the second-oldest daughter, Esther. The role gave her the chance to record soon-to-be-classics "The Trolley Song"—which was nominated for an Oscar—"The Boy Next Door" and "Have Yourself a Merry Little Christmas." Garland sings the latter tune to her on-screen sister Tootie (Margaret O'Brien) during a pivotal moment when the Smith family plans on leaving their Missouri home for New York City. The song is meant to be comforting, to relay that even if life separates us from friends and loved ones, the goodbye isn't forever—just temporary.

These three songs are credited to the songwriting team of Ralph Blane and Hugh Martin, who sang together in a vocal quartet and later wrote for movies and musicals. According to a 1989 NPR interview, "Have Yourself a Merry Little Christmas" almost didn't happen. "I found a little madrigal-like tune that I liked but couldn't make work," Martin said then, "so I played with it for two or three days and then threw it in the wastebasket." Blane, however, assured his partner the song was good—and encouraged him to fish the song out of the trash. (In his 2010 memoir *Hugh Martin: The Boy Next*

Door, Martin raised questions about the provenance of "Have Yourself a Merry Little Christmas" and other music from *Meet Me in St. Louis*; Blane, he claimed, didn't write the music or lyrics to these songs and other compositions credited to the pair.)

There were initially other issues with "Have Yourself a Merry Little Christmas," Martin recalled—namely that Garland and the movie's producers thought the song was too much of a downer. At first, he also wasn't keen on making changes. "[Garland] said, 'If I sing that, little Margaret will cry and they'll think I'm a monster,'" Martin recalled to NPR in 2006. "So I was young then and kind of arrogant, and I said, 'Well, I'm sorry you don't like it, Judy, but that's the way it is, and I don't really want to write a new lyric.'"

He eventually acquiesced to these requests, although any changes didn't diminish the emotional ache at the center of "Have Yourself a Merry Little Christmas." Garland's vocal delivery is reassuring and heartfelt, while also being wholly sympathetic to her sister's sorrow. Although she's the older sibling attempting to keep a stiff upper lip, she lets her own grief and sadness slip through, making her performance that much more relatable.

Garland's "Have Yourself a Merry Little Christmas" eventually performed modestly on the charts. Over the years, however, other takes on the song have become more common. Frank Sinatra covered the song on his 1957 LP *A Jolly Christmas from Frank Sinatra* and released the song again in 1963. The version from 1957 is crisp and resigned, with grandeur that comes from a cooing choir and a lush orchestra. And in 2022, Michael Bublé's equally debonair cover of the song even charted on the *Billboard* Hot 100.

THE CHRISTMAS SONG

1946 • NAT KING COLE

Songwriters: Mel Tormé and Robert Wells
Also covered by: Christina Aguilera, Jacob Collier, Perry Como, Mel Tormé

THE MOST MEMORABLE Christmases often don't involve grand gestures. Instead, over time, you'll fondly remember the way beloved annual traditions add up and result in an unforgettable holiday. On "The Christmas Song," Mel Tormé and his writing partner Robert Wells vividly capture Christmas coziness—a chilly wind, a jolly choir, tasty roasted chestnuts—as well as the excitement of kids waiting for Santa Claus. The tune's denouement is just as sweet: The narrator sincerely wishes everyone, young and old, a merry Christmas.

The songwriters penned the tune on an "excessively hot afternoon" in July 1945, Tormé recalled in his autobiography, *It Wasn't All Velvet.* He had traveled to Wells's house in Toluca Lake for a writing session and happened to spot a poem on the piano that referenced Christmas carols, roasting chestnuts, and people bundled up to ward off winter's chill. When asked about the lyrics, Wells cited the hot weather and reportedly told Tormé, "I thought I'd write something to cool myself off. All I could think of was Christmas and cold weather."

Inspired, the pair buckled down to write and polished off "The Christmas Song" in just 45 minutes. Wasting no time, Tormé remembered they immediately took the tune to Hollywood and played it for their boss and other important people—including Nat King Cole, who liked the song enough to record it the following year not once but twice.

Although Cole cut both takes at New York City's WMCA Radio Studios, the two versions couldn't be more different. Recorded on June 19, 1946, the earlier version was contemplative, hewing toward meditative jazz, and featured Cole on vocals and piano accompanied by guitarist Oscar Moore and bassist Johnny Miller. (Incredibly enough, this take was unreleased until 1989, when it emerged accidentally on a compilation.)

Two months later, on August 19, 1946, Cole took another crack at "The Christmas Song." The second version featured the same trio configuration, plus nuanced drumming accents from Jack "The Bear" Parker, as well as soaring strings and a delicate harp. These flourishes add elegance that complements Cole's ornate piano and velvety vocal performance. Listening to "The Christmas Song," you feel like you're sitting by a roaring fire with family, enjoying each other's company and having a perfect night.

Issued under the name the King Cole Trio and featuring the parenthetical "Merry Christmas to You," the single reached the top 10 of *Billboard*'s radio airplay and retail charts in 1946. However, in a case of trying to improve upon perfection, Cole rerecorded the song several times, making subtle changes along the way. Notable composer Nelson Riddle contributed orchestral arrangements on the 1953 version, while the 1961 take was recorded in stereo. Other versions of "The Christmas Song" also later emerged with the parenthetical "Chestnuts Roasting on an Open Fire" in the title, so its identity is clear.

In a nod to Cole's versatility, these rerecords all had their unique merits and earned plaudits. For example, the 1946 version was inducted into the Grammy Hall of Fame in 1974, while the Library of Congress chose the 1961 version of "The Christmas Song" for its National Recording Registry in 2022.

JINGLE BELLS

1946 • FRANK SINATRA

Songwriter: James Lord Pierpont
Also covered by: Celtic Woman, Bing Crosby, Benny Goodman
and His Orchestra, Kimberley Locke

IF YOU RATED the jolliness of Christmas songs on a scale of one to ten, "Jingle Bells" would be at least an eleven. With its buoyant tempo and idyllic description of speeding through the snow on a sleigh while giggling your head off, the song exudes giddy exuberance and the sheer unfettered joy of the holiday season.

Believe it or not, however, "Jingle Bells" was reportedly written to commemorate Thanksgiving, not Christmas. And that's not the only quirk of the song: While it's a fact that James Lord Pierpont wrote "Jingle Bells" in the 19th century, exactly when and where he wrote the tune is a matter of contentious debate. Sheet music for a Pierpont song called "The One Horse Open Sleigh" was published on September 16, 1857. However, the city of Medford, Massachusetts, has a plaque noting that he wrote the song in 1850 at the Simpson Tavern, a fact verified by one Mrs. Otis Waterman. Historians know that races like the one described in the song also took place near Medford.

However, Pierpont moved to Georgia and served as the music director at the Unitarian Universalist Church in Savannah during the 1850s. As a result, the church also claims "Jingle Bells" as their own, noting on their website that they are "called the 'Jingle Bells' church" and displaying a plaque stating that Pierpont wrote the song during his tenure working there.

At any rate, musicians started cutting the song in the 1880s. Some versions of the song feature a verse that describes the ride going off the rails (literally) due to

a horse that guided the sleigh into a snowbank. The solution was to get a different, sleeker horse that could travel at faster rates of speed. Frank Sinatra omitted those extra verses, although he still made "Jingle Bells" his own, first recording the tune on August 8, 1946, in Los Angeles with the Ken Lane Singers and Axel Stordahl and His Orchestra. Appropriately, this version—which also appeared on Sinatra's iconic 1948 LP, *Christmas Songs by Sinatra*—is laid-back and cool, as if the Rat Pack ringleader were narrating the sleigh ride live from a chic jazz lounge while holding a martini.

Gordon Jenkins arranged another famous Sinatra version of "Jingle Bells." The Missouri native started reading music while still a toddler; in a 2021 interview with the radio station KMOX, Jenkins's son said his dad was tickling the ivories at the downtown St. Louis department store Famous-Barr by age seven. Jenkins later arranged music for luminaries such as Nat King Cole, Judy Garland, and Louis Armstrong, although his most famous work came with Sinatra. He won a Grammy Award for arranging "It Was a Very Good Year" and also conducted the 1957 version of "Jingle Bells," released on the LP *A Jolly Christmas from Frank Sinatra*. This version is even cooler, as it features a red-hot jazzy choir spelling out the title of the song and an even peppier vocal performance from Sinatra.

Incredibly enough, "Jingle Bells" reached the top 40 on the *Billboard* Hot 100 for the first time ever during the first week of 2022, when Sinatra's 1946 version peaked at No. 33. This also marked Sinatra's first appearance on this particular chart since 1980, when he made the cut with "Theme from New York, New York."

HERE COMES SANTA CLAUS (DOWN SANTA CLAUS LANE)

1947 · GENE AUTRY

Songwriters: Gene Autry and Oakley Haldeman
Also covered by: Mariah Carey, Doris Day, Billy Idol, Willie Nelson

NEXT TO BING CROSBY and Frank Sinatra, the other king of Christmas music in the pre–rock 'n' roll era was Gene Autry. This wasn't necessarily an obvious path for the actor and musician nicknamed the "Singing Cowboy." The Texas native cut his teeth starring in Western films in the 1930s and 1940s while launching a successful country music career with hits such as "Back in the Saddle Again" and becoming a beloved radio star.

However, Autry co-wrote one of the most enduring Christmas songs of all time, "Here Comes Santa Claus (Down Santa Claus Lane)." Jaunty and brisk, the jingle bell–heavy tune is a showcase for Autry's easygoing vocal delivery—charmingly, he pronounces Santa's name with a prominent twang—and a message of inclusion: The jolly gift-giver loves all kids, so if you behave and prepare for his arrival, Santa won't disappoint.

Autry was inspired to write "Here Comes Santa Claus (Down Santa Claus Lane)" thanks to a memorable experience during a holiday parade. In 1946, he hopped on his horse, Champion, and rode in the annual Santa Claus Lane Parade on Hollywood Boulevard. According to liner notes published in the hits collection *Sing, Cowboy, Sing!: The Gene Autry Collection*, Autry saw kids grinning and shouting "Here comes Santa Claus!" as he loped down the parade route.

The festive scene set his creative gears in motion and he started workshopping a song based on his experience. Autry then passed on his work in progress to the music publisher head Oakley Haldeman and an A&R man named "Uncle" Art Satherley. As described in the 2007 book *Gene Autry: His Life and Career*, the men took Autry's source material and ran with it, convening a convivial poolside dinner gathering on a sweltering summer night to punch up the song. (Among the attendees was a friend of Satherly's named Harriet Melka, who ended up receiving songwriting credit on the original shellac single release.) Future Country Music Hall of Fame inductee Johnny Bond recorded a demo of "Here Comes Santa Claus (Down Santa Claus Lane)" in his home studio the next day, setting the stage for Autry to then record the song on August 28, 1947.

"Here Comes Santa Claus (Down Santa Claus Lane)" reached the top 10 of *Billboard*'s Best-Selling Popular Retail Records chart months later, cementing Autry's status as a Christmas icon. Although his biggest seasonal hit would be 1949's "Rudolph, the Red-Nosed Reindeer," Autry would also later put his spin on "Up on the Housetop" and "Frosty the Snowman," and even branch out into other holidays, releasing an Easter song called "Peter Cottontail" in 1950. However, Autry is a staple of *Billboard*'s annual Holiday 100 chart for his Christmas oeuvre; in 2022, no less than three of his festive tunes graced the chart. "Here Comes Santa Claus (Down Santa Claus Lane)," meanwhile, reached a new peak of No. 25 on the *Billboard* Hot 100 that same year.

RUDOLPH, THE RED-NOSED REINDEER

1949 • GENE AUTRY

Songwriter: Johnny Marks
Also covered by: Bing Crosby, Burl Ives, the Temptations

EVERYONE ROOTS FOR an underdog. And in the holiday universe, fewer underdogs are more beloved than Rudolph, the Red-Nosed Reindeer. Mocked and excluded for looking different (by his fellow reindeers, no less!), Rudolph eventually saves Christmas. You see, his ruddy nose shone brightly enough to cut through the gloom of a foggy Christmas Eve night, making him the perfect choice to lead Santa's sleigh around the world, so the jolly one can deliver presents. Predictably, Rudolph's bullies then realize the error of their ways, change their tune, and start calling Rudolph a legend.

The irrepressible reindeer was the creation of Robert Lewis May, who worked in advertising for the department store Montgomery Ward and was known around the office for writing parodies. During the 1939 holiday season, store execs commissioned May to write a lighthearted children's story, as part of a promotional campaign to draw parents in to buy toys. Working at night and on weekends, May took inspiration from the premise of the underdog-does-good story "The Ugly Duckling" and created Rudolph.

The combination of this well-crafted tale and whimsical illustrations by a coworker made Rudolph a sensation. Montgomery Ward gave away 2.4 million free copies of the 32-page story in 1939. The gambit was so successful that the store reprinted the Rudolph story in 1946 and distributed another 3.6 million copies. May also earned the copyright for his creation, which led to an audio version of the story released on an LP and a hardcover version of his tale.

However, he was committed to making Rudolph even more popular—and more lucrative. "Along with newspaper and magazine articles, radio and TV interviews, I thought of trying to accomplish my purpose with a Rudolph song," May wrote in a 1976 letter to the son of the former Montgomery Ward president, Wilbur H. Norton.

Rudolph's plight interested noted holiday song hitmaker Johnny Marks, who reportedly read the book while deployed during World War II and liked the title enough to tuck it away for future songwriting inspiration. (In another telling of this origin story, May asked Marks to write the song directly; as it turns out, Marks was also married to May's sister.) Marks put together a song that preserved the spirit of May's original story; this tune was subsequently recorded by actor and musician Gene Autry in June 1949.

Incredibly enough, Autry was initially reluctant to record the song, but agreed to at the urging of his wife, Ina, who noticed the parallels to "The Ugly Duckling" and (correctly) saw the tune's appeal. Autry recruited his frequent radio show collaborators the Pinafores—a musical and vocal trio comprising sisters Eunice, Beulah, and Ione Kettle—and added light orchestral flourishes. The resulting twang-kissed song felt like a bedtime story, with Autry's rich voice reciting the lyrics over jaunty, string-punctuated melodies.

"Rudolph, the Red-Nosed Reindeer" became a commercial smash, hitting No. 1 on both *Billboard*'s Best-Selling Pop Singles chart and the DJ-driven Country & Western chart in early 1950. Autry subsequently clearly warmed up to the song, as he rerecorded it in 1957 with a lusher orchestral accompaniment. And, just as May had hoped, Rudolph grew into a beloved holiday staple, not only because of the song but also media like the groundbreaking 1964 Rankin/Bass TV special *Rudolph the Red-Nosed Reindeer*, which was made using stop-motion animation.

BABY, IT'S COLD OUTSIDE

1949 • ELLA FITZGERALD & LOUIS JORDAN

Songwriter: Frank Loesser
Also covered by: Kelly Clarkson and John Legend, Doris Day and Bob Hope, Amy Grant and Vince Gill, Dolly Parton and Rod Stewart

IF YOU'RE A BROADWAY composer responsible for legendary musicals such as *Guys and Dolls* and *How to Succeed in Business Without Really Trying*, chances are good you're going to write a dynamic and dramatic Christmas song. In the case of Frank Loesser—who won a Tony for the former and nabbed a Grammy and shared the Pulitzer Prize for Drama for the latter—that holiday classic was "Baby, It's Cold Outside."

Although the song has drawn controversy in the modern age, its origins are much more innocuous. According to Loesser's daughter, Susan, her dad wrote the song for her mom, Lynn Garland, who had musical talent of her own. "It was 1944 and my father wrote it because when he and my mom had parties, everybody had to have an act to entertain the guests," Susan Loesser told NBC News in 2018, while noting that "flirting was a whole different thing back then."

With that context in mind, "Baby, It's Cold Outside" indeed feels like a mini-play, where two people are bantering back and forth about what direction a snowy night is going to take. One half of the couple attempts to leave, fretting over what people might think if they are spotted; the other person tries to persuade the reluctant party to stay, dangling things like a drink and a warm home as temptation. The lyrical push-and-pull is thick with romantic tension and innuendo that can be interpreted as unwanted pressure, although elements of the phrasing do exhibit the flirtatiousness referenced by Loesser's daughter.

Frank Loesser eventually sold "Baby, It's Cold Outside" to MGM, which used the song twice in the 1949 film *Neptune's Daughter*. Lynn Garland, the songwriter's wife, was reportedly quite unhappy about the sale. However, the song won an Oscar for Best Original Song and it was enormously popular: In 1949 alone, nine versions of "Baby, It's Cold Outside" made a cultural impact. One of these, by Ella Fitzgerald and Louis Jordan, has minimal instrumentation from Jordan's band, the Tympany Five. Instead, the two vocalists carry the song, taking a lighthearted approach to the lyrics; Jordan especially oozes charm, based on a wink and a smile in his voice.

In the modern world, particularly after the #MeToo movement that brought issues of sexual misconduct to the cultural forefront, the lyrical content of "Baby, It's Cold Outside" hasn't been viewed as favorably. During the 2018 holiday season, radio stations in Cleveland and San Francisco even decided not to play the song in response to listeners' wishes.

Interestingly enough, this reaction wasn't new: Even during the 1940s, "Baby, It's Cold Outside" raised eyebrows. *Time* magazine dug up a 1949 article from their vaults about the song that noted, "Queasy NBC first banned the lyrics as too racy, then decided they contained nothing provably prurient, and put the tune on the air." In a nod to these content concerns, Kelly Clarkson and John Legend updated the lyrics to the song on their 2019 cover, softening the pressure for the woman to stay and adding in language that makes it clear the woman is making her own decisions.

MELE KALIKIMAKA (MERRY CHRISTMAS)

1950 • BING CROSBY & THE ANDREWS SISTERS

Songwriter: R. Alex Anderson
Also covered by: Dead Meadow, Don Ho,
Kacey Musgraves, Poi Dog Pondering

BING CROSBY BECAME a Christmas music legend due to his World War II–era classics "White Christmas" and "I'll Be Home for Christmas." In turn, the success of these songs gave him freedom to pick and choose what holiday songs he wanted to record. In 1950, Crosby decided to cut a breezy tune called "Mele Kalikimaka," which roughly translates to "Merry Christmas" in Hawaiian.

The laid-back song—which was written by R. Alex Anderson and released nearly a decade before Hawaii officially became a US state—conjures up a tropical locale. Most obvious are its gentle Hawaiian guitar flourishes, although the single also boasts soft, brushed percussion that suggests palm trees rustling in the wind and sudden brass swells that call to mind an ocean wave cresting on the beach. Although Crosby understandably took a somber vocal tone for his wartime Christmas songs, on "Mele Kalikimaka" he lightens up considerably; it's easy to imagine him singing the tune on a tranquil island as the sun sets.

Born in Honolulu in 1894, songwriter R. Alex Anderson wrote over 200 songs inspired by his home state, including "Lovely Hula Hands" and "Mele Kalikimaka." In a 1994 interview, Anderson explained that the idea for the latter song came to him via a stenographer with whom he worked. "She said, 'Mr. Anderson, how come [there are] no Hawaiian Christmas songs?'" he recalled. "She said, 'They take all the hymns

and they put Hawaiian words to the hymns, but there's no original melody.'" Inspired, Anderson took what she said to heart. "I thought this over, and over a period of a few days this came into my head, I put it down on paper, and I've been singing it ever since."

In what proved to be a smart move, Anderson played this song to his friend and golfing buddy—Bing Crosby. The singer loved "Mele Kalikimaka" so much that he recorded a version of the tune without telling Anderson in advance. On September 7, 1950, Crosby and the Andrews Sisters gathered with Vic Schoen and His Orchestra in a Los Angeles studio to record the single and its B-side, "Poppa Claus." The Andrews Sisters had been chart stars since the late 1930s and had recorded with Crosby quite a bit already, including on a hit cover of "Jingle Bells." Their sun-kissed vocal harmonies put "Mele Kalikimaka" over the top by adding both warmth and pep.

The song has appeared in films such as *National Lampoon's Christmas Vacation* and *Catch Me If You Can*. However, "Mele Kalikimaka" has also experienced a resurgence in recent years, even reaching as high as No. 25 on *Billboard*'s Holiday 100 chart.

FROSTY THE SNOWMAN

1950 • JIMMY DURANTE

Songwriters: Steve Nelson and Walter "Jack" Rollins
Also covered by: Gene Autry, Cocteau Twins, Jackson 5

AFTER WORLD WAR II ended and American soldiers returned home, the US experienced a baby boom. Perhaps that's one reason the late 1940s and early 1950s saw an uptick in singles and albums geared toward children. One of these kid-friendly songs, "Frosty the Snowman," was the creation of Walter "Jack" Rollins and Steve Nelson, the songwriting team behind the hop-tastic Easter song "Peter Cottontail."

The single is deceptively upbeat and stars Frosty the Snowman as a whimsical being who comes alive after wearing a magical top hat and has a blast making merry with kids. However, the tale takes a turn: Frosty realizes he's going to melt because it's

sunny and decides to wander off by himself so as not to make his new friends sad. The overarching message is to seize the day and have fun when you can—because you never know when unpleasant things might happen.

Despite its snowy setting, "Frosty the Snowman" was already being promoted in spring 1950. Perhaps that explains the song's immediate success and dominance, as multiple artists had a hit with "Frosty the Snowman" that year. Gene Autry, who was trying to duplicate the success of his previous smash, "Rudolph, the Red-Nosed Reindeer," took his version to the top 10 of both the country and pop charts. Both Nat King Cole and Guy Lombardo also graced the pop charts with a version of "Frosty the Snowman"; Nat King Cole's release even landed in the top 10. In addition, Roy Rogers, Red Foley, and Vaughn Monroe also covered the tune.

But it was renaissance man Jimmy Durante who recorded the most familiar and long-lasting version of "Frosty the Snowman." This endurance wasn't necessarily expected at the time: *Billboard* wrote a lukewarm review of Durante's 1950 take on the single, noting that it was "not likely to figure against strong competing sides, except among devout Duranteites." But by the time Durante recorded the song, he was already an established vaudeville, film, Broadway, and radio star. Plus, he also had musical experience; notably, he composed and sang the 1933 song "Inka Dinka Doo."

Durante's 1950 "Frosty the Snowman" approached the life and times of Frosty like a bedtime story. Buoyed by a lilting orchestra conducted by Roy Bargy, the tune finds the vocalist initially calling for kids to gather around him to listen to what he has to say. Durante then proceeds to share Frosty's ill-fated tale using a speak-sing vocal delivery that resembles a gruff teddy bear with a heart of gold. In his hands, the song has a bittersweet (if ultimately optimistic) vibe.

Fittingly, Durante later provided voice-over narration on the 1969 Rankin/Bass TV special *Frosty the Snowman*. He also rerecorded "Frosty the Snowman" for the special, perfecting his delivery so he comes across like a cigar-chomping bigwig, or a wizened newspaper editor sharing Frosty's story with authority.

SUZY SNOWFLAKE

1951 • ROSEMARY CLOONEY

Songwriters: Roy C. Bennett and Sid Tepper
Also covered by: Soul Coughing

ALTHOUGH SNOW IS a welcome sight on Christmas morning, that's not always the case when it comes to any other day of the season. However, the delightful "Suzy Snowflake" offers an enticing alternative: Maybe we would view these flurries differently if we thought of them as an actual person. More specifically, Suzy's an out-of-town guest coming to visit and have good times—helping build snowmen, making sleigh rides more fun, and spreading merry cheer to all.

"Suzy Snowflake" sprang from the imaginations of Roy C. Bennett and Sid Tepper, neighbors in Brooklyn who would go on to cowrite dozens of songs for Elvis Presley, as well as Cliff Richard and the Shadows' 1961 hit "The Young Ones." The pair found the perfect voice for Suzy in Rosemary Clooney, who had already amassed multiple hit singles in 1951, including the No. 1 hit "Come On-a My House."

As far as "Suzy Snowflake" was concerned, Clooney took the song's playful premise and ran with it. Her voice twinkles with glee as she relays Suzy's adventures, as if she were reliving her own childhood fun. *Billboard* took notice of this sparkle, writing in an October 20, 1951, review: "Miss Clooney gets off a smooth chanting job on as fine a winter song as has been heard in some time."

"Suzy Snowflake" was actually the B-side of Clooney's single "Little Red Riding Hood's Christmas Tree." However, both songs featured an orchestra led by Tony Mottola, a guitarist who later accompanied Ray Charles and Frank Sinatra and also served as a member of *The Tonight Show* Band. The group's accompaniment elevates the song's whimsy; for example, as Clooney mentions Suzy knocking on a window, a stern percussionist pounds out a beat in time to the lyric.

Despite its cleverness and the fact that Clooney re-cut the song in 1978, "Suzy Snowflake" didn't become a major chart hit or a major holiday staple. However, the song endures in other ways. In 1953, it spawned a beloved black-and-white stop-motion cartoon that's survived the decades and is available to watch on YouTube.

SANTA BABY

1953 • EARTHA KITT

Songwriters: Joan Javits and Philip Springer
Also covered by: Ariana Grande, Madonna, Kylie Minogue, Taylor Swift

WHEN IT COMES to songwriting, a great partnership can make magic. Take the sultry "Santa Baby," co-written by Joan Javits and Philip Springer. The former was on staff at the legendary Brill Building and notably wrote lyrics for the 1953 Eddy Arnold song "Second Fling," while the latter had written music for the 1950 Connie Haines hit "Teasin'." When the duo came together to write "Santa Baby," the result was electric—quite possibly the only Christmas song that's a jazzy, slow-burning seduction.

Javits and Springer co-wrote "Santa Baby" specifically for Eartha Kitt, who was then a Broadway favorite thanks to her tenure in the Katherine Dunham Troupe and had broken into music earlier in 1953 with the release of *RCA Victor Presents Eartha Kitt* and its hit single "*C'est si bon.*" In 2017, Springer told the *Los Angeles Times* he initially had doubts about the assignment because Kitt "is the sexiest woman in the world. You don't write Christmas songs that are sexy. How are we going to do that?" He added that the powers that be who had hired him for the writing gig weren't concerned and told him just to focus on his work.

With this worry set to the side, work began on the song. Javits came up with the song title and the duo settled in at the piano in Springer's Upper East Side apartment to start writing. Springer polished off the music quickly and then took his part to RCA Victor musical director Henri René, who crafted a tasteful-yet-teasing arrangement that fit Kitt's strengths. "I wish he was still alive, because I'd send him a big check," Springer told *Columbia* magazine in 2020.

Next, Javits reportedly spent three weeks honing the "Santa Baby" lyrics. She brought a female perspective to the words—rare for a holiday song—which no doubt explains why the song is so relatable and true to what it feels like to have a crush. A syndicated newspaper column even praised Javits by name, writing that "Santa Baby" is "good because of its words, which were written by a gal composer." "Santa Baby" is full of sly double entendres and references to luxury gifts the narrator would like Santa to bring: a convertible, a yacht, jewelry. Kitt makes it very clear that Santa is wrapped around her little finger, as she enunciates each syllable with purpose and draws out certain words and phrases, to irresistible effect.

Springer admitted to the *Los Angeles Times* that when he turned in "Santa Baby," he wasn't quite sure it hit the mark. Later in the interview, he noted that he thought he had written better songs that weren't as popular as "Santa Baby." He concluded that some things are simply a mystery: "The answer has to be that 'Santa Baby' has a magic that goes beyond a composer's plans."

I WANT A HIPPOPOTAMUS FOR CHRISTMAS

1953 • GAYLA PEEVEY

Songwriter: John Rox
Also covered by: LeAnn Rimes, The Three Stooges, Gretchen Wilson

THE POST–WORLD WAR II era was a golden age for Christmas songs geared toward children. In the case of 1953's "I Want a Hippopotamus for Christmas," the tune was even sung by a kid: 10-year-old Gayla Peevey. Hailing from Oklahoma, Peevey was a burgeoning child star at the time. That summer, she was chosen to appear as a featured singer on Hoagy Carmichael's national TV show *Saturday Night Revue* after well-received local appearances on the radio and a telethon.

Building on that momentum, Peevey cut "I Want a Hippopotamus for Christmas." The song was the brainchild of Iowa resident John Herring (aka John Rox), who had studied music in Vienna, Austria, and also wrote the song "It's a Big, Wide, Wonderful World" for the Broadway musical *All in Fun*. Accordingly, the musical backdrop of "I Want a Hippopotamus for Christmas" is a bold and strident marching band with prominent trilling flutes and majestic horns.

Peevey's voice is clear and confident, as if she's working overtime to convince her parents that she deserves the supersized gift, and she wields a sly sense of humor that aids her cause. For example, Peevey acknowledges a major parental concern—the hippo might view her as a snack—but then reassures her parents that she was taught in school that the hippo is a vegetarian.

That fall, Peevey promoted the song by appearing on *The Ed Sullivan Show*. More prominently, "I Want a Hippopotamus for Christmas" inspired a real-life push to make the song's titular wish come true. Fate (and some savvy promo work) was on Peevey's side: The Bronx Zoo in New York had a female hippo named Mathilda looking for a home, because she had been rejected by a potential mate named Pete. (A United Press story theorized that Pete was perhaps intimidated, since the 700-pound Mathilda weighed almost twice as much as he did.) Via an Oklahoma newspaper, people donated $4,000—a figure equivalent to more than $44,000 in 2023—to cover Mathilda's travel expenses to reach the Oklahoma City Zoo.

Peevey was on hand to greet the hippo, who flew overnight from New York City, nestled in a crate with comforts like hay and vegetables. Reports at the time noted that the young singer's family wasn't interested in having a hippo move in, so Mathilda settled in at the Oklahoma City Zoo instead and lived to be 48 years old.

In a 2017 NPR interview, Peevey admitted that she knew she was never going to get a hippo out of the promotion. "Of course, the zoo and the newspaper were sponsoring the fund and knew what the end result would be." She also revealed that she wasn't really a hippo fan before singing the song, although she had grown to love the animal and had become an advocate for hippo conservation. Peevey also had nothing but fond memories of "I Want a Hippopotamus for Christmas," she told NPR: "If I have any legacy, what more fun legacy than to have a song that makes people happy and children dance around and brings a little cheer to the season?"

(THERE'S NO PLACE LIKE) HOME FOR THE HOLIDAYS

1954 • PERRY COMO

Songwriters: Robert Allen (music); Al Stillman (lyrics)
Also covered by: Garth Brooks, the Carpenters, Robert Goulet, Hanson

MANY CHRISTMAS SONGS offer a simple message: Home is where the heart is happiest. Barber-turned-vocalist Perry Como conveyed this warm, fuzzy feeling in a 1954 song appropriately titled "(There's No Place Like) Home for the Holidays." Backed by Mitchell Ayres and His Orchestra—which contributes fizzy accompaniment that feels suited for a crowded big-band dance—Como captures the indefatigable joy of spending time with family.

In "(There's No Place Like) Home for the Holidays," the ritual of going home and seeing loved ones is just as rewarding as actually being there. The song's lyrics detail someone traveling from Tennessee to Pennsylvania, with the promise of pumpkin pie waiting at the end of the trip, and describe the joyful moment when you stand on the porch, ready to greet relatives at your destination. Even traffic jams can't dampen holiday happiness; the song keeps the singer's spirits up while he's stuck in gridlock.

"(There's No Place Like) Home for the Holidays," which is sometimes titled just "Home for the Holidays," was a production by the team of composer/pianist Robert Allen and lyricist Al Stillman. The pair had written songs for Como before, including 1953's "My One and Only Heart"; additionally, Allen had accompanied Como on piano.

On 1959's *Season's Greetings from Perry Como*, Como re-cut the song again with the Mitchell Ayres Orchestra and added the Ray Charles Singers. This take is a bit more solemn and introspective at first, as if the singer is mulling over past holidays, but then accelerates from a low-lit jazz number into what sounds like an upbeat musical revue. The differences in tone and tempo can be jarring—but in truth capture the whirlwind of a holiday celebration to a tee. Unsurprisingly, "(There's No Place Like) Home for the Holidays" remains a holiday favorite and appears annually on *Billboard*'s Holiday 100.

JINGLE BELL ROCK

1957 • BOBBY HELMS

Songwriters: Joseph Carleton Beal and James Ross Boothe
Also covered by: Daryl Hall & John Oates, Miranda Lambert and Blake Shelton, Rascal Flatts, George Strait

AS THE 1950s progressed, mainstream pop music started embracing the lively sounds of youth-oriented rock 'n' roll. Holiday music also followed suit, moving toward a more contemporary style geared toward kids and teens.

One of the earliest rock 'n' roll holiday success stories was "Jingle Bell Rock." Performed by Bobby Helms—a Bloomington, Indiana, native who was then a burgeoning country star—the single put a modern spin on traditional Christmas music. More specifically, the song envisions holiday season dancing and merrymaking in places like the outdoor Jingle Bell Square or on a cozy sleigh. Throughout the song, the word *jingle* connotes vibrant, youthful revelry—there's a reason it's called jingle bell rock and not, say, jingle bell waltz—with clever rhymes (including "mingle" with "jingle") that convey lighthearted scenes.

Articles from the time of the song's release noted that it was popular with teens, although not everyone was convinced that it conveyed holiday cheer. ("I can't quite fancy Santa Claus as a rock and roll addict!" wrote a *Portland Evening Express* critic.) Still, "Jingle Bell Rock" exudes a festive vibe that fits the season.

Helms had been discovered by the country music legend Ernest Tubb, and, prior to the release of "Jingle Bell Rock," had nabbed two country No. 1 hits in 1957, "Fraulein" and "My Special Angel." The holiday tune continues in this vein, with easygoing, twangy guitar licks meshing well with background vocals from Nashville session icons the Anita Kerr Singers. The vocalists, who had also appeared on "My Special Angel," punctuate Helms's crisp tongue-twisting before taking center stage on the bridge with cascading harmonies.

In terms of songwriting, "Jingle Bell Rock" is credited to Joseph Carleton Beal and James Ross Boothe. However, there is some disagreement over the song's origins. In a 1992 *Indianapolis Star* interview, Helms claimed "Jingle Bell Rock" emerged after he made significant changes to an existing tune. "I really didn't want to cut it because it was such a bad song," he said. "So one of the musicians [and I] worked on it for about an hour putting a melody to it and we put a bridge to it."

That other musician happened to be Hank Garland, a session guitarist who had played on Patsy Cline's "Walking After Midnight" and Brenda Lee's "Rockin' Around the Christmas Tree." In Garland's recollection, he and Helms were sent a song called "Jingle Bell Hop"—which does exist in song copyright databases, credited to Beal and Boothe—but declined to record it because they didn't like the quality. "I let it hop back to where it came from," Garland told the *Jacksonville Business Journal* in 2001.

In that same interview, Helms's manager, Dave Davis, affirmed that Garland and Helms worked up and recorded "Jingle Bell Rock" during the session that was supposed to yield the other, disliked tune. Davis believed the pair's composition had enough changes and additions to be considered a new song, which therefore should have earned them songwriting credit. To date, however, neither Helms nor Garland has received credit for "Jingle Bell Rock."

The song has only grown in popularity over the years. Back in 1957, the single, which was backed on its B-side by the awesomely titled obscurity "Captain Santa Claus (and His Reindeer Space Patrol)" reached the top 10 of *Billboard*'s Honor Roll of Hits and enjoyed country airplay. With appearances in 1996's Arnold Schwarzenegger and Sinbad comedy *Jingle All the Way*, as well as consistent radio airplay, "Jingle Bell Rock" ascended into the *Billboard* Hot 100's top 10 in 2018, an eye-popping 60 years after its initial chart debut, and reached No. 3 in 2022.

BLUE CHRISTMAS

1957 • ELVIS PRESLEY

Songwriters: Billy Hayes and Jay W. Johnson
Also covered by: Shakin' Stevens, Ernest Tubb,
Ann & Nancy Wilson, Billy Eckstine

ELVIS PRESLEY WASN'T the first artist to tackle "Blue Christmas." In fact, the song was popular even before the King of Rock & Roll put his stamp on it. Orchestra versions led by (respectively) Hugo Winterhalter and Russ Morgan graced *Billboard*'s Best-Selling Pop Singles chart in 1949. The following year, jazz-influenced pop singer Billy Eckstine cut the song, while a version by country legend Ernest Tubb reached No. 1 on *Billboard*'s Most-Played Juke Box (Country & Western) Records chart.

The Tubb version especially inspired Presley to cut his own version of "Blue Christmas." On September 5, 1957, Elvis recorded the song at LA's Radio Recorders studio during a three-day round of sessions that yielded music for his first full-length holiday release, *Elvis' Christmas Album.* The studio time came amid a landmark year for the hip-swiveling star, who experienced both pop and R&B success with the chart-topping singles "All Shook Up" and "(Let Me Be Your) Teddy Bear."

Enlisting his trusted musical collaborators—guitarist Scotty Moore, bassist Bill Black, and drummer D. J. Fontana—as well as notable Nashville singers the Jordanaires, Presley crafted an instantly classic slice of holiday heartbreak. In fact, he sounded like a natural to cover the song. His subdued, downtrodden voice positively trembles with sadness, as he warbles about how lonely his Christmas will be without his beloved. More specifically, everything about his holiday—the memories, the snowfall, his mood—will be blue, while his estranged honey will have a postcard-perfect white Christmas. The Jordanaires amplify his bummed-out emotional mood with sighing, swooping background vocals, and harmonies that ooze empathy.

Fittingly, "Blue Christmas" was inspired by a gloomy day. The writer Jay Johnson, known for penning scripts for radio shows, came up with the tune during a rainy commute from his hometown of Stamford, Connecticut, to New York City. According to the *Norwich (Connecticut) Bulletin*, Johnson "wondered why someone hadn't written a holiday song combining some blues into it," especially since there was a song called "White Christmas." He wrote down some initial ideas on hotel stationery and later hammered out the rest of the tune with a composer friend, Billy Hayes.

"Blue Christmas" appeared both on *Elvis' Christmas Album* and on a 1957 EP called *Elvis Sings Christmas Songs.* However, Presley also found sustained success with his take on "Blue Christmas." When the song was released as a single in 1964, it reached No. 1 on *Billboard*'s Holiday Singles chart. "Blue Christmas" also made the setlist of his legendary '68 Comeback Special. Presley's puppy-dog eyes and anguished vocal performance made the tune a highlight; it was clear the passage of time hadn't dulled the pain of spending a holiday alone. Today, "Blue Christmas" remains a popular part of the season—a song offering a thoughtful gift for the heartbroken, a salve to the soul in tough times. It even reached a new peak of No. 24 on the *Billboard* Hot 100 in early 2023.

RUN RUDOLPH RUN

1958 • CHUCK BERRY

Songwriters: Chuck Berry and Marvin Brodie
Also covered by: Bon Jovi, Sheryl Crow, Foghat, Keith Richards

IN 1958, Chuck Berry celebrated Christmas by hopping on a flight to New York City to connect with Alan Freed's Christmas Jubilee of Stars, a multi-show residency held at the Loew's State Theatre. Doors opened at 9 a.m. sharp for the all-day concert, which featured nonstop music and lived up to its billing: Joining Berry at various times during the week were Bo Diddley & Band, Jackie Wilson, Ritchie Valens, the Flamingos, Frankie Avalon, Eddie Cochran, the Everly Brothers, Johnnie Ray, Dion and the Belmonts, and many more.

Berry was closing out yet another successful year that saw him nab top 10 hits with "Johnny B. Goode" and "Sweet Little Sixteen." However, the holiday show appearance was especially timely: That December, he issued a Christmas song, "Run Rudolph Run," described by *Billboard* as "a rousing rock and roll effort about one of Santa's reindeer." The lighthearted song finds Rudolph tearing around at lightning-fast speeds to get presents for kids—an electric guitar for a boy, a doll that drinks and cries for a girl—and make Christmas special. Amusingly enough, the reindeer is encouraged to take the freeway (it's faster, you see) to get the job done—hence the encouragement to run.

According to Berry's self-titled 1987 autobiography, he recorded "Run Rudolph Run" on November 19, 1958, during the same session as another holiday tune ("Merry Christmas Baby") and two other songs: "Little Queenie" and "That's My Desire." The two Christmas songs appeared together on a seven-inch single issued by Chess Records. Like many other hits at the time, songwriting provenance eventually came into question. On the original pressing, Berry's music company is credited alongside one Marvin Brodie.

However, 1959 *Billboard* articles about the success of the songwriter Johnny Marks—the man credited with penning "Rudolph, the Red-Nosed Reindeer"—include "Run Rudolph Run" as being part of Marks's holiday song repertoire. On certain later pressings, the song was credited to Brodie and Marks, not Berry—a mistake perpetuated by the fact that the two men were also listed as songwriters on a 1978 "Run Rudolph Run" cover by Rolling Stones guitarist Keith Richards. To deepen the mystery, there's some question as to whether Marvin Brodie even exists. Vintage newspaper and magazine archives reference a Dr. Marvin Brodie who was a respected radiologist, and a behind-the-scenes record label employee named Marvin Brodie, but don't mention a songwriter.

A post on the Chuck Berry Collectors Blog quoted what was alleged to be a Facebook post by one-time Berry pianist Daryl Davis. In the post, Davis said he had a conversation with Berry about the songwriting confusion surrounding "Run Rudolph Run." Berry said he did indeed write the song—and claimed that a dispute over using the trademarked Rudolph image led to a lawsuit and the fictitious Brodie songwriting credit. The claim seems credible because, in hindsight, it's difficult to imagine anyone other than Berry writing "Run Rudolph Run." The song is classic Chuck and very reminiscent of his other songs of this era: He pairs plaintive, vibrant vocals and bluesy guitar riffs with upbeat musical accompaniment, namely rollicking piano and swinging drums.

"Run Rudolph Run" peaked at a modest No. 69 on the *Billboard* Hot 100 after its initial release in 1958. However, much like Berry himself, the song triumphantly duck-walked its way to holiday immortality, as it was certified platinum in November 2020 and reached No. 10 on the *Billboard* Hot 100 in early 2021—a whopping 62 years after it first graced the charts.

THE CHIPMUNK SONG

1958 • THE CHIPMUNKS WITH DAVID SEVILLE

Songwriter: Ross Bagdasarian (Sr.)
Also covered by: Del Rubio Triplets, Amy Grant,
Kacey Musgraves, Tegan and Sara

IN 1958, an actor and singer named Ross Bagdasarian (Sr.), recording under the name David Seville, had an unexpected pop smash with a quirky song called "Witch Doctor." Bagdasarian was no stranger to the charts: He previously co-wrote "Come On-a My House," which was a No. 1 song for Rosemary Clooney in 1951. However, "Witch Doctor" wasn't your typical wacky novelty. To make the song, Bagdasarian spent $200 (more than $2,000 in 2023) on a reel-to-reel cassette recorder and started experimenting with tape manipulation, pitch-shifting his voice to create a cartoonish character that recited the song's nursery rhyme–like chorus.

Bagdasarian struck gold again applying the same whimsical (and out-there) approach to "The Chipmunk Song," which is also known as "The Chipmunk Song (Christmas Don't Be Late)." A waltzing tempo and orchestration, bolstered by playful flourishes—an oompah horn, Spanish-inspired guitar—augment funny-sounding, high-pitched voices that are meant to represent chipmunks.

According to a 1960 *Teen* interview (quoted in the *Hollywood Reporter*), Bagdasarian came up with a melody for "The Chipmunk Song" first—because he couldn't read or write music, he whistled the part into a tape recorder—and then wrote lyrics. Next came a twist, he admitted: "[I] decided the singers should be animals or maybe even insects." After considering mice, rabbits, and (of all things) butterflies, he hit on the idea of having chipmunks be the singers.

The unexpected conceit worked like a charm. "The Chipmunk Song" is a meta song starring Bagdasarian-as-Seville as an exasperated narrator trying to wrangle three irrepressible chipmunks—Alvin, Simon, and Theodore—as they practice a Christmas tune. (The critters were named after executives from Bagdasarian's label, Liberty Records.) The trio trill about wanting a fancy toy plane and a hula hoop, and beg Christmas to arrive on time, ostensibly because they want their gifts to arrive faster.

Surprisingly, the chipmunks are initially resistant to singing, but by the end of the song, they're enthusiastically ready to perform "The Chipmunk Song" again and again. In a nod to Bagdasarian's skills and meticulous recording nature, the characters all have different personalities—Simon is clearly the responsible one, while Alvin is mischievous and seems distracted—and harmonize perfectly.

"The Chipmunk Song" started getting radio airplay even before Thanksgiving— then a rare occurrence—and quickly grew into a sales juggernaut. *Billboard* reported that Liberty was shipping 200,000 copies of the single per day in mid-December, and noted that the record was on track to sell 3 million copies, making it the highest-selling single since Elvis Presley's "Hound Dog." Unsurprisingly, the single reached No. 1 on *Billboard*'s Hot 100 *and* Honor Roll of Hits in late 1958, a position it would hold on both charts through early the following year. It also garnered three awards at the very first Grammy Awards, including Best Recording for Children and Best Comedy Performance.

Alvin & the Chipmunks, meanwhile, would grow into an enduring pop culture phenomenon, encompassing singles and albums, movies, a TV cartoon, and more. They wouldn't leave their Christmas roots behind, however: In 1960, they recorded a version of "Rudolph, the Red-Nosed Reindeer," while "The Chipmunk Song" was reissued several times and became a staple of later Chipmunks media, including 1961's *The Alvin Show*.

ROCKIN' AROUND THE CHRISTMAS TREE

1958 • BRENDA LEE

Songwriter: Johnny Marks
Also covered by: Alabama, Justin Bieber, Meghan Trainor, Kim Wilde

TEENAGERS IN THE LATE 1950s had no shortage of songs celebrating the joy of moving and grooving. Brenda Lee's "Rockin' Around the Christmas Tree" imagined how that spirit of fun applied to a festive holiday party. Couples surreptitiously dance toward the mistletoe, munch on some pumpkin pie, and go caroling; in fact, Lee even very pointedly references lyrics from the standard "Deck the Halls" to underscore the jolly atmosphere.

"Rockin' Around the Christmas Tree" wasn't Lee's first contribution to the holiday music canon. In 1956, she released the single "I'm Gonna Lasso Santa Claus" (backed by the B-side "Christy Christmas") to little success. However, "Rockin' Around the Christmas Tree" followed the musical trends of the time and had a solid pedigree: It was written by the holiday music dynamo Johnny Marks, the author of "Rudolph, the Red-Nosed Reindeer" and later the classic "A Holly Jolly Christmas."

In 2015, Lee recalled to the *Tennessean* that Marks specifically asked her to sing his tune. "I was only 12, and I had not had a lot of success in records, but for some reason he heard me and wanted me to do it." As it happens with many holiday songs, timing didn't align for her to record "Rockin' Around the Christmas Tree" during colder months. However, Lee noted that producer Owen Bradley provided a festive mood in the studio anyway, blasting air conditioning to mimic chilly winter air and installing a Christmas tree and lights.

Lee's vocal performance benefited from this setup, as she belts out lyrics like she's in the thick of a raucous party having a total blast. Additionally, the session featured a Who's Who of Nashville players: guitarists Hank Garland and Grady Martin; bassist Bob Moore; saxophonist Boots Randolph; pianist Floyd Cramer; and the Anita Kerr Singers. These players also bring a party vibe to the song, in the form of jovial guitar licks, upbeat harmonies, and a boisterous sax solo.

With such a supportive environment, "Rockin' Around the Christmas Tree" was destined to become a success. And it did—eventually. Although the tune didn't connect upon its initial release in 1958 *or* 1959, it did finally take its place as a holiday classic in 1960, which coincided with Lee earning two US No. 1 pop singles, "I'm Sorry" and "I Want to Be Wanted."

"Rockin' Around the Christmas Tree" has only become more beloved in the ensuing decades. Lee has cited the song's appearance in the 1990 movie *Home Alone* as a turning point, telling the *Tennessean* that the Macaulay Culkin holiday film "breathed new life" into the tune. "It has just been a blessing." In fact, Lee's tune even ascended to No. 1 on *Billboard*'s Holiday Airplay chart in 2019 and No. 2 on the *Billboard* Hot 100 in 2022.

LET IT SNOW! LET IT SNOW! LET IT SNOW!

1959 • DEAN MARTIN

Songwriters: Sammy Cahn and Jule Styne
Also covered by: Carly Simon, Jessica Simpson, Frank Sinatra, Rod Stewart

IT WOULD BE LOGICAL to assume that inspiration for holiday music typically arrives during colder months. But, incredibly enough, many songwriters instead get into the Christmas spirit during warmer months. In fact, a July 1945 heat wave in Los Angeles, yielded not one but at least *two* legendary Christmas songs. The first was the Nat King Cole–popularized Mel Tormé–Robert Wells composition "The Christmas Song" (see page 26). The other was "Let It Snow! Let It Snow! Let It Snow!" by the decorated songwriting team of Sammy Cahn and Jule Styne.

In 1945, Cahn and Styne were early in what would become legendary careers. Among their many highlights: Styne composed music for Broadway showstoppers "Don't Rain on My Parade," "Diamonds Are a Girl's Best Friend," and "Everything's Coming Up Roses," while lyricist Cahn won four Oscars and penned the words for songs like "Love and Marriage." (Many know the latter tune as the *Married . . . With Children* theme song.) Together, the two men also had great artistic chemistry, winning the 1954 Oscar for Best Original Song for the Frank Sinatra tune "Three Coins in the Fountain."

Their creative mind-meld surfaced once again on the day "Let It Snow! Let It Snow! Let It Snow!" started percolating. "It was one of the hottest days in the history of Los Angeles," Cahn recalled in his 1989 book, *Sammy Cahn's Rhyming Dictionary*, and the pair had just finished a meeting. "I asked Jule, 'Why don't we drive to the beach to cool off?' He said, typically, 'Why don't we stay here and write a winter song?' " Cahn headed to a typewriter and banged out the first four lines of the song. Inspired, Styne sat at the piano and started noodling around to find a melody that fit the rhyming words.

When all was said and done, the men came up with a flirty and romantic song that follows a lovey-dovey couple who cuddle up next to a fire and enjoy each other's company, while a snowstorm rages. They're perfectly fine with the flurries flying outside; after all, inside it's warm and cozy. Even when one-half of the couple moves to go home—after an extended good-bye, of course—the memory of this perfect night wards off a chill from the frosty air.

Appropriately enough, crooner Dean Martin recorded "Let It Snow! Let It Snow! Let It Snow!" for his 1959 LP *A Winter Romance*. The session date? The dog days of summer: August 6, 1959. Backed by a trilling orchestra, he beat the heat with a chic take on the song that oozed sophistication. Martin later re-cut "Let It Snow! Let It Snow! Let It Snow!" for 1966's *The Dean Martin Christmas Album*, and the song has gone on to become a holiday classic; it even reached No. 8 on the *Billboard* Hot 100 in late 2020. Still, it was far from the only time "Let It Snow! Let It Snow! Let It Snow!" graced the pop charts. For example, in early 1946, Vaughn Monroe had a massive hit with the song for RCA Victor with a version that reached No. 1 on *Billboard*'s Records Most-Played on the Air chart.

LITTLE SAINT NICK

1963 • THE BEACH BOYS

Songwriters: Brian Wilson and Mike Love
Also covered by: Captain & Tennille, John Denver and
the Muppets, Rosie Flores, Straight No Chaser

EVERYBODY KNOWS Santa Claus is one of the hippest dudes out there. After all, he flies around on a sleigh and brings everybody in the world presents on Christmas. How could Santa possibly get any cooler than that? On "Little Saint Nick," the Beach Boys' Brian Wilson had an idea: Give the jolly man a different set of wheels. More specifically, the song imagines Santa steering a supercharged, bright-red vehicle that boasts plenty of horsepower. The ever-affable, patient rein-

deer gang keep up with their speedy leader, ensuring that Christmas comes off without a hitch.

Envisioning a daredevil Santa joyriding in a flashy car was almost edgy for the Beach Boys during the early 1960s. The band touted the cool cars and pretty girls of sun-kissed California through fresh-faced hits such as "Little Deuce Coupe" and "Surfer Girl." However, "Little Saint Nick" shows off their heavenly familial harmonies and melodic genius. Stray vocal counterpoints and lyrics pop out of the candy cane–sweet music, underscoring the song's plot highlights.

Ever the musical trendspotter, Brian Wilson wrote the Beach Boys' Christmas song partly because of Phil Spector's 1963 holiday album. Inspiration struck at an unexpected moment, he said in the book *Becoming the Beach Boys, 1961–1963*: "I wrote the lyrics to it while I was out on a date and then I rushed home to finish the music." (Mike Love, Wilson's cousin and fellow Beach Boys member, was added to "Little Saint Nick" as a cowriter in the 1990s after a lawsuit over songwriting credits.)

The Beach Boys cut the vocal and instrumental parts of "Little Saint Nick" in October 1963, adding twinkling, percussion-like sleigh bells and glockenspiel for seasonal flair. At the same time, the group also recorded the single's B-side, a lovely a cappella version of "The Lord's Prayer." Separately, the group included another version of "Little Saint Nick" on their hit 1964 full-length *The Beach Boys' Christmas Album* that has the same twirling tempo and heavenly vocals, but possesses subtle differences from the original single, mainly that it doesn't include the sleigh bells and other chiming percussion.

That wasn't the only time the Beach Boys tweaked "Little Saint Nick." There's also an alternate version of the song based on the instrumental parts of a song called "Drive-In," recorded the year before—this take boasts a more rock 'n' roll vibe, with a brisker tempo and different lyrics—and a 1991 remix of the song. However, "Little Saint Nick" was a hit to begin with—it reached No. 3 on *Billboard*'s Christmas Singles chart in 1963—and remains a beloved part of holiday music lore today. In early 2023, the song reached a new peak of No. 29 on the *Billboard* Hot 100, giving the Beach Boys their first Top 40 hit since 1988's "Kokomo."

CHRISTMAS (BABY PLEASE COME HOME)

1963 • DARLENE LOVE

Songwriters: Jeff Barry, Ellie Greenwich, Phil Spector
Also covered by: Mariah Carey, U2

CLASSIC CHRISTMAS SINGLES abound in popular culture, although it's much less common to come across a classic holiday LP. A major exception is *A Christmas Gift for You from Phil Spector*. Released in 1963 and produced by Phil Spector, it features the Ronettes, the Crystals, and Darlene Love, as well as accompaniment from instrumental icons the Wrecking Crew. As a result, the liner notes contain some staggering names; to name a few, pianist Leon Russell, drummer Hal Blaine, and arranger Jack Nitzsche. A very young Cher even sang on every song, with her musical partner Sonny Bono contributing percussion.

Today, *A Christmas Gift for You from Phil Spector*'s most famous song is Love's "Christmas (Baby Please Come Home)." With its twinkling percussion, shimmering vocal harmonies, and sugar-spun instrumentation, the song feels like the soundtrack to a gorgeous, powdery snowfall. (Paradoxically, Love recorded "Christmas [Baby Please Come Home]" during a sweltering summer heat wave, although Spector kept the studio chilly enough that wearing sweaters during the session was a must.) A brief fuzzy sax solo cuts through the music, adding twinges of melancholy and longing.

"Christmas (Baby Please Come Home)" is dominated by a powerhouse, anguished vocal performance from Love, who as a member of girl-group the Blossoms sang lead on the 1962 hit "He's a Rebel." (The latter song is credited to the Crystals, but the voice is unmistakably Love's.) She urges a beloved to come

home and reminisces about all the good times they've had in the past, although it's unclear whether the person is gone permanently—say, after a breakup or on a faraway trip—or has just left temporarily, like after a fight.

Despite the song's emotional heft, Love said in a 2019 podcast interview that she and two of the song's writers, the legendary team of Jeff Barry and Ellie Greenwich, were at first wary about releasing a new and original Christmas tune, instead of a tried-and-true, proven song. "But Phil was determined," Love said. "He said, 'It's a great song, you got to hear it.' And they actually played the song for me over the phone." Hearing this demo changed Love's mind, and she was all-in, she added. "I thought it was going to be a great song."

The album was released initially under the name *A Christmas Gift for You From Phillies Records*, in a nod to Spector's label, Phillies. Surprisingly, the LP wasn't a hit at first and neither was "Christmas (Baby Please Come Home)." (To date, a non-holiday version of the song, called "Johnny (Baby, Please Come Home)," which emerged in 1977 as a B-side, also hasn't made much of a dent.) Over time, however, both Love's song and the LP have become an integral part of the holiday season.

From 1986 onward, Love would make an annual guest appearance on David Letterman's late-night talk show and perform the song. Her appearances were always a joy, as they overflowed with all the trimmings: jubilant choirs, a mini-orchestra, a saxophonist dressed like Santa. "That song means something to everybody [who] hears it," Love said on the podcast. "So you get really joyful when you're singing."

SLEIGH RIDE

1963 • THE RONETTES

Songwriters: Leroy Anderson (music); Mitchell Parish (lyrics)
Also covered by: Mariah Carey, Ella Fitzgerald, Gwen Stefani

IN ADDITION TO original songs, *A Christmas Gift for You from Phil Spector* also included beloved, time-tested holiday chestnuts such as "White Christmas" and "Silent Night." The Ronettes, a girl group from New York City led by the irrepressible Ronnie Spector, also chimed in with covers of "Frosty the Snowman," "I Saw Mommy Kissing Santa Claus," and "Sleigh Ride."

"Sleigh Ride" was originally an instrumental song composed by Leroy Anderson, a military translator and interpreter who spoke nine languages and held a master's degree in music from Harvard. Somewhat incongruously, he came up with the idea for "Sleigh Ride" in the hot summer months of 1946. The Boston Pops and its legendary conductor Arthur Fiedler eventually premiered "Sleigh Ride" in May 1948, several months after Anderson finally finished the song. Mitchell Parish—a renowned lyricist known for standards such as "Stardust" and "Moonlight Serenade"—only added lyrics to "Sleigh Ride" in 1950. His words were simple but effective, capturing the chilly fun of hopping on a sleigh and going on a delightful romp through an idyllic snowscape with your honey.

The Ronettes seize the vibe of this spirited wintry fun on "Sleigh Ride," in no small part because Ronnie Spector was always a huge fan of the holiday season. In a 2019 interview with *Billboard*, she detailed fond childhood Christmas memories: watching ice skaters at Radio City Music Hall, gazing adoringly at department store windows, seeing Santa Claus. That pure joy and delight permeates every aspect of the song. After setting the scene with clattering hooves and horse whinnies, "Sleigh Ride" sails forward on a sizzling, jazzy rhythm augmented by pirouetting strings, staccato sax, and jingling percussion. The Ronettes make the song even more their own by supporting the lead melody throughout with stacked backing vocals that echo and mimic the chiming sound that bells make. In the hands of the group, "Sleigh Ride" feels like a whirlwind romantic adventure, suited for a postcard-perfect fairy tale.

The Ronettes' "Sleigh Ride" has remained an indelible part of the holiday season, as it's been included in countless movies and TV shows. Spector herself also never lost her appreciation for both this song and other Ronettes holiday tunes: "When I get in my car and hear 'Sleigh Ride' and 'Frosty the Snowman,' I get goose pimples," she told *Billboard*. "When I'm driving, I pull over just to hear my songs." In a fitting tribute, in early 2022, just weeks before Ronnie Spector passed away, the Ronettes' "Sleigh Ride" reached a new peak of No. 10 on the *Billboard* Hot 100—meaning the song is now the group's second-biggest US chart hit after "Be My Baby."

CHRISTMAS TIME IS HERE

1963 • VINCE GUARALDI TRIO

Songwriters: Vince Guaraldi (music); Lee Mendelson (lyrics)
Also covered by: Debby Boone, Chicago, John Pizzarelli, R.E.M.

IN THE 1965 animated television special *A Charlie Brown Christmas*, earnest Charlie Brown teaches everyone the true meaning of Christmas—not presents or perfect decorations, but friendship, family, and fellowship. An evocative soundtrack, composed by jazz pianist Vince Guaraldi, makes the special even more meaningful, as the music captures the special's many moods—whimsy, melancholy, joy, determination.

Lee Mendelson, who executive-produced *A Charlie Brown Christmas*, initially picked Guaraldi to write music for a Peanuts documentary after hearing the pianist's 1963 top 40 hit "Cast Your Fate to the Wind." "Something in my mind said, 'That's the kind of music that I'm looking for,'" Mendelson said in an interview with PRI's Studio 360. "It's adult-like, but also child-like. It seemed to fit our characters."

The documentary, *A Boy Named Charlie Brown*, never aired on TV, although the film did spawn a 1964 Vince Guaraldi Trio LP, *Jazz Impressions of "A Boy Named Charlie Brown."* Mendelson was pleased enough with the work to have Guaraldi compose music for a Peanuts Christmas special. The results exceeded his already high expectations, as the subsequent *A Charlie Brown Christmas* soundtrack—which Guaraldi once again recorded as a trio, with drummer Jerry Granelli and bassist Fred Marshall—spawned many indelible tunes, including the upbeat, fleet-footed "Linus & Lucy."

However, Guaraldi had also written another instrumental song, the meditative "Christmas Time Is Here," that ended up being used as the special's opening theme. Mendelson loved the song's melody and wanted to add lyrics but couldn't find anyone for the job. "So I sat down with an envelope—I'll never forget this—at our kitchen table and wrote 'Christmas Time Is Here' in about 10 minutes," he told PRI's Studio 360. "It was a poem that just came to me—never changed the words to this day."

He didn't need to: Sung by a chorus of angelic-voiced kids and propelled by plaintive piano and gentle brushed percussion that sounded like someone trudging through the snow, the song struck the right emotional chord. Mendelson's sentimental lyrics reinforced the themes of the TV special: The true meaning of Christmas is everywhere around us, generated by gathering with your family, singing Christmas carols together, and watching kids have an absolute blast.

It's not a stretch to say that *A Charlie Brown Christmas* was many people's first exposure to jazz music. And today, both the soundtrack and the TV special *A Charlie Brown Christmas* remain illuminating holiday staples for kids of all ages. In fact, Guaraldi earned his second-ever top 40 hit, nearly 60 years after his first one, when "Linus & Lucy" reached No. 37 on *Billboard*'s Hot 100 in 2021.

IT'S THE MOST WONDERFUL TIME OF THE YEAR

1963 • ANDY WILLIAMS

Songwriters: Edward Pola and George Wyle
Also covered by: BarlowGirl, Harry Connick Jr., Amy Grant, Johnny Mathis

YOU MIGHT SAY Andy Williams's "It's the Most Wonderful Time of the Year" functions as a checklist for how to have a great holiday season. After proclaiming the season's greatness, the song ticks off various activities (e.g., caroling, roasting marshmallows, kissing under mistletoe, sharing ghost stories) that add up to a fun holiday. To underscore the grand nature of the season, "It's the Most Wonderful Time of the Year" boasts contributions from a bold and brassy orchestra, with arrangements by Johnny Mandel—a noted composer who would later write the music for the *M*A*S*H*

theme "Suicide Is Painless"—and dramatic backing vocals.

"It's the Most Wonderful Time of the Year" was co-written by Edward Pola and George Wyle. Both men wrote multiple songs together, including ones cut by Doris Day and Bing Crosby, although Wyle detoured into unexpected (and fascinating) places by himself as the 1960s and

1970s progressed. He co-wrote the theme song for the beloved TV shipwreck sitcom *Gilligan's Island* and was also musical director of *The Flip Wilson Show* and the Christmas special *John Denver and the Muppets: A Christmas Together.*

Wyle prepped for this TV work by serving as choral director on *The Andy Williams Show.* In a 2005 interview with the Television Academy Foundation, Williams recalled that Wyle "wrote all of the choir stuff and all of the duets, trios, and things that I did with the guests" and penned "It's the Most Wonderful Time of the Year" specifically for the show's 1962 Christmas-themed special. "I did that every Christmas, and then other people started doing it, and over 30 years, it's become a big standard."

It helped, of course, that Williams was a show business veteran by the time *The Andy Williams Show* went on the air in 1962—among other things, he was a regular presence on *Tonight Starring Steve Allen* and had been a recording artist since the late 1940s, even earning a No. 1 hit in 1957 with the song "Butterfly." He knew how to bring the right amount of showbiz flair to make the song a hit.

The version of "It's the Most Wonderful Time of the Year" Williams released in 1963 became a holiday favorite that now crashes the *Billboard* Hot 100 annually. In 2021, it reached a new peak of No. 5. A cover of "It's the Most Wonderful Time of the Year" by Johnny Mathis is also popular and was used to particularly great effect in the film *Jingle All the Way.* "It's the Most Wonderful Time of the Year" has also found new life in advertisements and lighthearted TV appearances, like the time actress Mindy Kaling teamed up with the Muppets for a version.

A HOLLY JOLLY CHRISTMAS

1965 • BURL IVES

Songwriter: Johnny Marks
Also covered by: Michael Bublé, Alan Jackson, Lady A

WHY WISH SOMEONE "Merry Christmas!" when you could wish them "A Holly Jolly Christmas"? That's the premise of Burl Ives's jaunty single, which encourages people to put on their merriest demeanor when heading out into the world during the holidays. That might involve smooching with your sweetheart if you spot mistletoe, or simply waving hello and sending good tidings to friends you see while out and about. Over time, "A Holly Jolly Christmas" has become one of the most popular Christmas songs. In fact, it reached No. 4 on the *Billboard* Hot 100 in 2021 and No. 3 on the list of Top 25 ASCAP Holiday Songs that same year.

"A Holly Jolly Christmas" had a distinct advantage right from the start, as the tune was written by a Christmas music songwriter with a Midas touch: Johnny Marks, the man who had also penned "Rudolph, the Red-Nosed Reindeer" and "Rockin' Around the Christmas Tree." As it so happens, "A Holly Jolly Christmas" appeared in the 1964 Rankin/Bass animated TV special *Rudolph the Red-Nosed Reindeer,* in which Marks was involved. Ives was part of the special, too, narrating as the distinguished, mustache-sporting Sam the Snowman and singing several Marks songs, including "A Holly Jolly Christmas."

None of this was accidental. According to a November 1964 *Hartford Courant* feature, Marks suggested "A Holly Jolly Christmas" to both Ives and his label, Decca Records, and persuaded the singer to record the song. For good measure, Marks also convinced General Electric, which sponsored the TV special, to hire Ives to portray Sam the Snowman. Understandably, the renowned songwriter added that he was immensely proud of his work on *Rudolph the Red-Nosed Reindeer.* "I think I've written the greatest songs I've ever done in my life for this show," Marks said. "This year I'm going all-out to push 'A Holly Jolly Christmas,' thanks to Burl's record."

Rudolph the Red-Nosed Reindeer wasn't Ives's first show business rodeo, either. Prior to "A Holly Jolly Christmas," he had already cultivated a lengthy career that included winning an Academy Award for Best Supporting Actor (for his role in 1958's Western film *The Big Country*) and dabbling in folk and country music. His version of "A Holly Jolly Christmas," heard on the TV special, is brisk and no-nonsense: Driven by taut orchestral spirals and the occasional auxiliary choral flourish, the song feels as though Ives is commanding people to have a happy holiday.

The more familiar version of "A Holly Jolly Christmas" found on Ives's 1965 holiday album, *Have a Holly Jolly Christmas*, hews closer to his country music roots. Buoyed by kicky acoustic guitar and a slower tempo, the take is more laid-back and jubilant. Owen Bradley, who previously helmed Brenda Lee's "Rockin' Around the Christmas Tree," directed the orchestra and chorus on "A Holly Jolly Christmas," which also helped lighten the mood; the backing vocals especially added a friendly, joyous tone.

YOU'RE A MEAN ONE, MR. GRINCH

1966 • THURL RAVENSCROFT

Songwriters: Theodor Geisel (lyrics); Albert Hague (music)
Also covered by: *The Glee* cast, Lindsey Stirling,
Tyler, the Creator, the Whirling Dervishes

THERE'S AN OLD SAYING that goes, "One bad apple spoils the whole bunch." With apologies to the 1966 animated TV special *Dr. Seuss' How the Grinch Stole Christmas!*, perhaps the more appropriate saying is "One evil Grinch spoils the whole Christmas holiday." Based on the Dr. Seuss book of the same name, and narrated by the debonair actor Boris Karloff, the TV special stars a shaggy-haired, lime green–colored, devious creature who is hell-bent on ruining Christmas for the population of Whoville. Disguised as Santa Claus, the Grinch steals presents and decorations and intends to throw them away. Eventually, however, seeing the spirit of Christmas in Whoville melts his grumpy façade and he reluctantly embraces the holiday.

Naturally, the Grinch had his own clever theme song, "You're a Mean One, Mr. Grinch," with music by Albert Hague, lyrics by Theodor Geisel (aka Dr. Seuss) and vocals by Thurl Ravenscroft. Hague was a veteran Broadway composer who later went on to portray a music teacher in the TV series and movie *Fame*. Ravenscroft, meanwhile, was a deep-voiced vocalist with close ties to Disney—notably, he was part of the chorus singing "Pink Elephants on Parade" in the movie *Dumbo* and provided voice-over for the theme park's Pirates of the Caribbean ride—and was the robust voice and personality of Frosted Flakes cereal star Tony the Tiger for more than a half-century.

"There probably wasn't a time where we were not out in public where somebody would come up to him and say, 'Do I know you? You sound so familiar,'" Ravenscroft's daughter, Nancy Snope, said in a 2018 radio interview. "And dad would say, 'Does the word 'great' mean anything?'"

That anonymity occasionally backfired on Ravenscroft; in fact, he wasn't officially credited as singing "You're a Mean One, Mr. Grinch." However, his stern and foreboding baritone voice was perfect for the song, as he drawled the outlandish descriptions of the Grinch's personality—a soul full of garlic, a cactus-prickly personality, a rotten banana—in a tone that's both playful and pointed. A lively orchestra emphasizes these vivid images and the Grinch's sneaky personality, in the form of over-the-top brass parts and restrained strings.

"You're a Mean One, Mr. Grinch" appeared on the 1966 soundtrack to *Dr. Seuss' How the Grinch Stole Christmas!* alongside several other originals. The LP won the Grammy Award for Best Recording for Children. The TV special still airs to this day, while the book also spawned a 2000 live-action film starring Jim Carrey as the Grinch. As for Ravenscroft, although he wasn't initially associated with the song, he's since received heaps of praise for his performance as the song grew into a holiday staple. In 2021, "You're a Mean One, Mr. Grinch" even made the US *Billboard* top 40.

CHRISTMAS TIME (IS HERE AGAIN)

1967 • THE BEATLES

Songwriters: George Harrison, John Lennon, Paul McCartney, Ringo Starr
Also covered by: R.E.M.

BACK IN THE DAY, joining the fan club of your favorite band was a way to receive exclusive gifts. For members of the Beatles' fan club, Christmas meant receiving a seven-inch record that featured music and holiday greetings from the Fab Four. These releases aren't quite as well-known as other Beatles records, but they do offer glimpses into the band's collective sense of humor and show off the group's free-spirited side.

The first Beatles fan club record arrived in 1963 and set the tone for the rest of the series. The quartet do a silly version of "Good King Wenceslas," featuring jokey lyrics and falsetto voices, and then the individual band members contribute goofy (but gratitude-filled) words about the preceding blockbuster year.

Four years later, the Beatles were significantly more famous but also far more skilled studio musicians. Released in 1967, "Christmas Time (Is Here Again)"—also billed as "The Beatles Fifth Christmas Record"—is lighthearted but also much slicker. The single leans in the psychedelic rock direction of 1967's "Strawberry Fields Forever," as it's dominated by a simple chorus repeating the title of the song over and over again. In between this music, band members intersperse high-concept comedic skits—fake ads for fake products, dramatic spoofs of BBC newscasts—and drummer Ringo Starr repeatedly spelling the word *out*. The vibe ends up somewhere between surreal and slapstick, with music that sounds expertly produced and arranged.

"Christmas Time (Is Here Again)" is notable for being credited to all four Beatles, a rarity within the band's catalog. It was also the last fan club release the four members of the band recorded together; each Beatle recorded their contributions for the final two singles in the series separately. According to the website The Beatles Bible, the recording session for "Christmas Time (Is Here Again)" took place on November 28, 1967, in Studio Three at the band's preferred locale: London's EMI Studios on Abbey Road. At the time, the Beatles had just wrapped up the *Magical Mystery Tour* LP and would soon travel to India to study transcendental meditation, a trip that helped shape their ambitious double LP, *The White Album*. The session for "Christmas Time (Is Here Again)" started at 6 p.m. and went into the wee hours of the following day. In addition to including the Beatles, the session featured producer George Martin and an actor named Victor Spinetti; the latter also ended up on the tune.

Unless you were a card-carrying member of the Beatles fan club, the original 1967 version of "Christmas Time (Is Here Again)" remained difficult to find until it became more widely available on a 2017 boxed set, *Happy Christmas Beatle People! (The Christmas Records)*, which compiled the Fab Four's original Christmas records. However, over the years, the song surfaced via bootlegs and in other forms. A different version of "Christmas Time (Is Here Again)" appeared on the flip side of the Beatles' 1995 single "Free as a Bird." Starr also did a solo version on his 1999 Christmas album, *I Wanna Be Santa Claus*. That cut featured Aerosmith's Joe Perry adding a very George Harrison–esque guitar solo and Ringo reprising his spelling lesson with gusto.

WHAT CHRISTMAS MEANS TO ME

1967 • STEVIE WONDER

Songwriters: Anna Gordy Gaye, George Gordy, Allen Story
Also covered by: En Vogue, Al Green, Hanson, John Legend

WHEN STEVIE WONDER released his first Christmas album, 1967's *Someday at Christmas*, he was just 17 years old. By this time, however, he already had several hits under his belt, including the virtuosic "Fingertips," the soul/R&B strut "Uptight (Everything's Alright)," and the smoldering "I Was Made to Love Her." His label, Motown Records, also had a solid track record for holiday albums, having released *Christmas with the Miracles* in 1963 and, two years later, the Supremes' *Merry Christmas*.

Recorded in Detroit during the summer of 1967, *Someday at Christmas* features Wonder's interpretations of select covers ("Ave Maria," "Silver Bells"), but mainly includes originals, like the politically pointed title track. However, the album's most heartwarming moment is the final song on side two: "What Christmas Means to Me." Lyrically, the song expresses gratitude for all the trappings that make the holiday great—flickering candles, snow, mistletoe, carolers—but circles back to one meaningful thing: romance with a special someone. Wonder sings of wanting to experience everything Christmas has to offer (kissing under the mistletoe, decorating the tree, decking the halls, waking up early) with his sweetie.

"What Christmas Means to Me" was co-produced by a pair of Motown associates: Harvey Fuqua—who cofounded the Moonglows and later worked in A&R and as a label producer—and songwriter/future recording artist Johnny

Bristol. The song was also co-written by three people with strong ties to Motown Records: Anna Gordy Gaye, George Gordy, and Allen Story.

Story penned songs for many of Motown's biggest stars in addition to Wonder, including the Temptations and Diana Ross and the Supremes. George Gordy was the brother of Motown Records founder Berry Gordy. And Anna Gordy Gaye—sister of George and Berry Gordy—cofounded Anna Records, the label that distributed Barrett Strong's 1960 hit "Money (That's What I Want)" across the US. Anna was also a Motown songwriter; among her co-written compositions were several songs on *What's Going On*, the seminal LP by her one-time husband Marvin Gaye.

With this background and experience, the trio knew exactly how to write a song that suited Wonder's strengths. Augmented by brilliant instrumentation—rumbling bass, jubilant horns, and saltshaker sleigh bells—the musician sings effusively, positively shouting the song's lyrics he's so excited by their sentiments. Like an upbeat punctuation mark on the proceedings, Wonder then unfurls one of his inimitable, honey-smooth harmonica solos as the song winds down, adding a beatific feeling that lingers after the music ends.

Billboard praised *Someday at Christmas* in a review, noting that, "By combining traditional and newer material, Stevie Wonder has come up with an intense, moving package." But despite this praise—and the fact that the title track reached the magazine's Best-Selling Christmas Singles chart in 1966—the album didn't chart in the US. In fact, *Someday at Christmas* reached its peak of No. 34 on the *Billboard* Top Holiday Albums chart only in early 2021. "What Christmas Means to Me" also initially didn't make much of an impact after being issued as a single in 1971 but earned a spot on the legendary 1973 compilation *A Motown Christmas* and has since become a popular song to cover.

SANTA CLAUS GO STRAIGHT TO THE GHETTO

1968 • JAMES BROWN

Songwriters: Hank Ballard, Charles Bobbit, Alfred "Pee Wee" Ellis
Also covered by: Anthony Hamilton

IN THE US, 1968 was a pivotal year. For starters, civil rights activist Reverend Martin Luther King Jr. was assassinated in April. This violent act led to riots in many major cities, and propelled conversations about racial oppression and discrimination to the cultural forefront. Among other things, two Black American Olympic athletes, Tommie Smith and John Carlos, took a stand against discrimination by raising their fists on the podium during "The Star-Spangled Banner" while receiving their medals. Smith told *Smithsonian* magazine the peaceful protest was "a cry for freedom and for human rights. We had to be seen because we couldn't be heard."

Unsurprisingly, this racial reckoning permeated the music made by funk and soul legend James Brown in 1968. His strutting, horn-peppered two-part single "Say It Loud—I'm Black and I'm Proud" was a No. 1 R&B hit and crossed over to the pop charts. Both parts of the tune also appeared on his 1968 holiday album, *A Soulful Christmas*, which featured a string of originals, including one called "Santa Claus Go Straight to the Ghetto."

The song was co-written by saxophonist and Brown band member Alfred "Pee Wee" Ellis, Hank Ballard—a member of the influential rock 'n' roll group the Midnighters; he's credited with writing "The Twist"—and Brown's manager

Charles Bobbit. More meditative and midtempo than other tunes from the icon—but with the kind of taut, tight grooves, and sonic punctuation marks for which Brown's band was known—it's a plea for Santa Claus to make sure to visit the neighborhoods that

might be forgotten. The song's lyrics stress that Santa should bring toys to kids—and calls them by name, even, so there's no mistaking who gets what—and points out that the families and residents need Christmas cheer. Vocally, Brown employs a gravelly, reverential vocal tone, reinforcing the song's important message.

"Santa Claus Go Straight to the Ghetto" had a major impact beyond the LP as well. Brown appeared on the December 26, 1968, cover of *Jet* magazine wearing a Santa hat. An accompanying feature story detailed his charity work, including benefits he played for Black organizations and how he planned to give gift certificates to 3,000 families in need that Christmas. "My people put me on top," he said in the interview. "I owe them for what I am today. Nothing I can do to help Black people will be too much."

SILENT NIGHT

1968 • THE TEMPTATIONS

Songwriter: Josef Mohr (lyrics); Franz Xaver Gruber (music)
Also covered by: Mariah Carey, Sinéad O'Connor, Elvis Presley, Percy Sledge

THE TEMPTATIONS WERE one of the biggest artists on Motown's label. Formed in 1960, the Detroit-based vocal group braided together harmonies and velvet-lined vocals on golden hits such as "My Girl" and "Ain't Too Proud to Beg." Naturally, the Temptations were well-suited for vocal-rich Christmas songs like "Silent Night." Produced by Norman Whitfield, the group's version of the song first appeared on 1968's *Merry Christmas from Motown*, a compilation that also featured Diana Ross & the Supremes, Stevie Wonder, and Smokey Robinson & the Miracles.

With lead vocals by Eddie Kendricks, the Temptations' "Silent Night" feels like a comforting church hymn. Kendricks's falsetto-leaning tenor adds sweetness to the lyrics, which honor the holiday's more religious overtones, and the gentle music. It's both reverent and restrained, while acting as a perfect example of the Temptations'

strengths as a vocal ensemble.

Technically, "Silent Night" is one of the oldest Christmas songs. A Catholic priest named Josef Mohr wrote the words to a poem called "*Stille Nacht*" in 1816, in the Austrian community Mariapfarr. Two years later, a flood damaged the organ at Mohr's church, St. Nicholas in Oberndorf bei Salzburg, putting the music at Christmas Eve mass in jeopardy. Luckily, the priest had an ace up his sleeve: The church's organist, Franz Xaver Gruber, who had some skill with musical composition, quickly arranged a piece of music for guitar and two vocalists, and the men performed the song at that evening's mass. Multiple articles note that, at the time, guitars were banned from being used in church, so the musicians performed the newly minted "Silent Night! Holy Night!" (or "Stille Nacht! Heilige Nacht!") later in the service.

Oberndorf bei Salzburg remains proud of its role in facilitating the creation of an enduring Christmas classic. Today, there's an attraction known as the Silent Night Chapel on the site where the song was first performed. According to local lore, Mohr's skull is even embedded within the building—a slightly macabre twist for such a meaningful song.

In modern times, "Silent Night" is more wholesome, thanks to covers by acts like the Temptations. The group later included their spin on "Silent Night" on 1970's *The Temptations Christmas Card*, which reached the top 10 on *Billboard*'s Christmas LPs chart the year of its release. In subsequent years, the Temptations appeared on TV performing the song and also re-cut the song several times; one version featured a lullaby-like intro and someone reciting verses from "'Twas the Night Before Christmas," while another boasted a sparser arrangement that emphasized strings over other instruments.

MERRY CHRISTMAS, DARLING

1970 • THE CARPENTERS

Songwriters: Richard Carpenter (music); Frank Pooler (lyrics)
Also covered by: Amy Grant, Lea Michele, Lennon Stella

THE EARLY 1970s were a golden age for original Christmas music, as established acts and new stars alike put a unique stamp on holiday cheer. Siblings act the Carpenters—vocalist/drummer Karen and her older brother, composer/instrumentalist Richard—were responsible for one of the biggest new holiday tunes of the decade: the lovelorn "Merry Christmas, Darling."

The song describes the sadder side of Christmas: the longing and heartache that often creeps in during quieter moments, after the hustle and bustle of the holidays subsides. A roaring fire in the fireplace reminds the song's narrator of a loved one who isn't there. As a result, they fervently wish their absent crush has a good Christmas *and* (for good measure) a happy new year. More than that, however, the protagonist wishes they could be together—although it's abundantly clear this is merely a dream.

"Merry Christmas, Darling" dates from the mid-1940s, when a man named Frank Pooler wrote the song as a Christmas gift for the girl with whom he was smitten. "I was 18 and the hormones were raging," he told the *La Crosse (Wisconsin) Tribune* in 2005. Unfortunately, the romance fizzled out, although he did get a 78 RPM album cut with the song for posterity.

Fast-forward two decades later and Pooler was working as the choral director at California State University–Long Beach. Two of his students, the Carpenter siblings, asked if he had any leads on a unique Christmas song they could perform.

Pooler dug out his song and gave it to Richard. A fastidious musical composer and arranger, the student crafted a different melody.

Several years later, Richard summoned Pooler to the A&M studio to hear something. "He sat me down and pulled a switch and these great sounds came out of the speaker," Pooler recalled. Much to his surprise and delight, it was the Carpenters doing his song, "Merry Christmas, Darling." Released in 1970, the single was a holiday hit, in no small part because the Carpenters had a breakthrough year, with the No. 1 smash "(They Long to Be) Close to You" and the equally huge hit "We've Only Just Begun."

"Merry Christmas, Darling" exemplifies what the Carpenters do best: lush, orchestrated pop music that strikes a deep emotional chord. Strings burble and bloom in the background of the song behind whispery drums and jazzy piano—a plush foundation for Karen Carpenter to contribute an elegant, wistful vocal performance. The vocalist also sings a lovely rerecorded version of "Merry Christmas, Darling" in the duo's 1978 TV special *The Carpenters: A Christmas Portrait*, crooning the song as fake snow falls softly around her. However, the original version graces *Billboard*'s holiday charts every year—a touching reminder of heartaches and losses that never quite fade away entirely, only recede from view.

FELIZ NAVIDAD

1970 • JOSÉ FELICIANO

Songwriter: José Feliciano
Also covered by: BTS, Celine Dion, Kacey Musgraves

SOMETIMES THE SIMPLEST gestures end up meaning much more than elaborate ones. The same goes for holiday songs—just ask José Feliciano, whose 1970 hit "Feliz Navidad" is a concise song that offers heartfelt "Merry Christmas!" greetings in both English and Spanish. The bilingual lyrics were by design—Feliciano knew this would give the song wider appeal, particularly on the radio—although he also wanted to capture an inclusive celebratory spirit. "My thought when I wrote the song was that it didn't matter what language you were singing in," he told the Associated Press in 2020. "The feeling of Christmas is privy to all of us."

Feliciano had a taste of success prior to releasing "Feliz Navidad." He reached No. 3 on the *Billboard* Hot 100 in 1968 with a cover of the Doors' "Light My Fire," leading him to win a Grammy that same year for Best New Artist. Feliciano then released a steady string of singles, although none came close to reaching this peak. That was partly because the soul-influenced version of the US national anthem he performed at the 1968 World Series didn't sit right with many people, Feliciano told NPR in 2020. "I had to leave America and play in other countries because I wasn't getting any radio play after I did 'The Star-Spangled Banner.'"

However, Feliciano persevered and, two years later, found himself in a Los Angeles recording studio working on music. He was missing his large family back in Puerto Rico—he had 10 brothers—and their annual Christmas Eve revelry included special food and drinks, and caroling in Puerto Rican celebrations known as parrandas. These comforting memories, coupled with homesickness, inspired him to write a song. "It was expressing the joy that I felt on Christmas and the fact that I felt very lonely," Feliciano told NPR. "I missed my family, I missed Christmas carols with them. I missed the whole Christmas scene."

Produced by Rick Jarrard, "Feliz Navidad" translates these feelings into what feels a lot like a colorful sonic celebration. Feliciano plays the guitar and a 10-stringed instrument called the cuatro, as a whirlwind of piercing strings swirl around him. Above all, his voice exudes sincerity and genuine emotion; when he notes that his holiday greetings are from the heart, there's absolutely no doubt that his intentions are pure and true.

"Feliz Navidad" appeared on Feliciano's 1970 Christmas album, which peaked at a modest No. 54 on the US album charts. However, the festive song has become one of the most popular holiday hits. Feliciano, for one, marveled at the song's endurance during a 2020 appearance on NBC's *Today*. "For some reason, this little song has united everyone. Nobody can get angry that you made them sing 'Feliz Navidad' because it's in Spanish. Nobody can get angry because you made them sing the English part."

To mark the 50th anniversary of "Feliz Navidad" in 2020, Feliciano re-cut the song with dozens of guest artists, including Styx, Sam Moore, Jason Mraz, Lin-Manuel Miranda, and Gloria Gaynor. In both 2021 and 2022, the original version of the song even reached the top 10 of *Billboard*'s Hot 100. As it turns out, Feliciano's message has continued to resonate loud and clear across the decades.

THIS CHRISTMAS

1970 • DONNY HATHAWAY

Songwriters: Donny Hathaway (music); Nadine McKinnor (lyrics)
Also covered by: Michael McDonald, Seal, Chris Stapleton
and H.E.R., the Whispers

DONNY HATHAWAY'S recording career was tragically brief, spanning a little over a decade before his death in 1979. Within that time frame, however, the soul icon—who was a gifted musician, songwriter, arranger, composer, and producer—accomplished quite a bit. He earned multiple R&B and pop hits with Roberta Flack and contributed Hammond organ to Aretha Franklin's 1972 classic LP *Young, Gifted and Black*. As a solo artist, the Chicago native also found a supportive audience with his 1970 solo LP, *Everything Is Everything*, and a self-titled 1971 album.

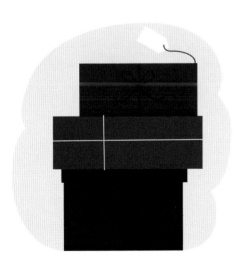

"This Christmas" arrived in between the release of these two full-lengths and illustrated why Hathaway deserved far more popularity. His voice is smooth as polished marble but warm and intimate; in fact, it sounds as though he's crooning the tune directly to someone else. The lyrics for "This Christmas" came courtesy of a Chicago postal worker named Nadine McKinnor. She connected with Hathaway thanks to a boyfriend who happened to be working in an office where the musician had his operations. In a stroke of luck, the boyfriend heard a discussion about Hathaway needing new music and recommended McKinnor.

Speaking to the *Chicago Tribune* in 2017, McKinnor explained that her lyrics were "trying to capture the swirl of music, department store windows, lights on the South Side—Chicago at Christmas." However, McKinnor viewed this specific inspiration as a window into more universal sentiments. "It's like I'm talking about a love affair with the atmosphere of the holiday," she continued. "My kids were little then, I was out shopping for toys, enjoying the mood. It's a romance with the season."

It's easy to hear why "This Christmas" resonated so deeply, as McKinnor's lyrics exude the fuzzy warmth of the Christmas season, especially when this time is spent with a loved one. "This Christmas" describes decorating a tree, placing mistletoe, receiving cards and presents, going caroling—a recipe for an ideal holiday. Seeing her lyrics come to life in the studio was magic, she recalled in 2017. "Watching Donny work was like watching a designer, someone who weaved threads and colors, though here [he was using] sounds and chord changes."

Hathaway recorded "This Christmas" in Chicago at Audio Finishers Studio, with a band that included an all-star group of musicians: his close collaborator, the guitarist Phil Upchurch; drummer Morris Jennings; baritone saxophonist Willie Henderson; future Earth, Wind & Fire trombonist Louis Satterfield; and, on percussion, Hathaway's business partner and co-producer, Ric Powell. Strings, meanwhile, came courtesy of members of the Chicago Symphony Orchestra—and Hathaway himself played a keyboard bass.

The result is classic '70s soul, overflowing with heart. "'This Christmas' is absolutely the premiere holiday song written by an African American," Upchurch told the *Chicago Sun-Times* in 2009. "Nothing comes close." *Billboard* named "This Christmas" one of its Christmas Picks of 1971, although the single didn't have much of an impact until years after Hathaway's 1979 death. It appeared on a 1991 reissue of the ATCO Records compilation *Soul Christmas* and has only gained more respect and admiration in the decades since.

In 2022, Rhino Records released a new version of "This Christmas," featuring Hathaway's daughter, Lalah, duetting with her father on a previously unheard 1970 demo of the song. This take is quite different; among other things, it's more laid-back and Donny Hathaway plays acoustic piano, which gives the song a gentler, funkier vibe. Lalah was ecstatic about the song, releasing a statement about the duet that read, "I am so honored to have my first recording with my dad be 'This Christmas'!!! I hope this means as much to you as it means to my family!"

SANTA CLAUS IS COMIN' TO TOWN

1970 • THE JACKSON 5

Songwriters: J. Fred Coots (music); Haven Gillespie (lyrics)
Also covered by: The Four Seasons, Dolly Parton, Bruce Springsteen, Sufjan Stevens

IN THE EARLY 1970S, few groups were more popular than the Jackson 5. Hailing from Gary, Indiana, the group featured five talented siblings—Jackie, Tito, Jermaine, Marlon, and Michael—who boasted an abundance of vocal and dance talent. Starting with 1969's "I Want You Back," the Jackson 5's first four singles on Motown Records reached No. 1 on the pop charts.

"Santa Claus Is Comin' to Town," which arrived directly after this string of chart-toppers, also hit No. 1 on *Billboard*'s Christmas Singles chart in late 1970. It's easy to hear why: The song soars on the strength of giddy vocals from

12-year-old Michael Jackson. The tween peppers his lively singing with some improvised "Oh yeahs," as his brothers chime in with some well-placed a cappella harmonies. Although some people interpret the song's lyrics as ominous— children are warned to be good because Santa is an omniscient, Big Brother–like figure—Jackson seems genuinely excited about Jolly Old Saint Nick swooping in to make the holiday great.

J. Fred Coots and Haven Gillespie co-wrote "Santa Claus Is Comin' to Town" in 1934. A Covington, Kentucky, native, Gillespie was a newspaper printer with big songwriting aspirations and previously earned hits when others cut his songs, such as "In the Harbor of Love with You" and "Drifting and Dreaming." However, Gillespie entered pop culture immortality due to a commission from a music publisher, which needed a Christmas song for the upcoming holiday season right away—no exaggeration, since the songwriting ask reportedly came on October 15.

Gillespie was still reeling from the recent death of his brother Irwin, but he was up to the challenge. "He didn't feel Christmasy," his nephew, William First, said in a 1994 interview with the *Tampa Bay Times*, "but the publisher offered good terms and promised all [kinds] of promotion." In New York City, Gillespie hopped on the subway in hopes of finding inspiration, which ended up being a smart move. Drawing from things his mother used to say about Santa keeping a close eye on him and his siblings, as well as other fond childhood memories, Gillespie crafted the rhyme-heavy lyrics to "Santa Claus Is Comin' to Town" on the back of an envelope during the ride. Coots—a Songwriters Hall of Fame member due to his work on Broadway and in Hollywood—added music soon after and the rest is history.

"Santa Claus Is Comin' to Town" became an immediate sensation in 1934. Mega-popular radio personality Eddie Cantor—who co-wrote "Merrily We Roll Along," aka the theme song of the *Merrie Melodies* cartoons—did a version of the song on his show. (Reportedly, he was initially hesitant but changed his mind because his wife, Ida, liked the song.) That same year, Harry Reser & His Orchestra and George Hall & the Hotel Taft Orchestra also both cut jaunty versions, while newspapers across the US reported that the song popped up as part of local holiday performances.

Unsurprisingly, in the December 29, 1934, issue of *Billboard*, "Santa Claus Is Comin' to Town" was No. 1 on the best-selling sheet music list, beating such classics as "Winter Wonderland." The song quickly became a perennial, sustained hit. In 1974, several years after the Jackson 5's rendition of the song, the Associated Press reported that "Santa Claus Is Comin' to Town" had sold 40.6 million records and 690,000 copies of sheet music. More than that, though, the tune has remained popular to this day—because while times and trends change, both anticipation for the holiday season *and* being excited about a visit from Santa never go out of style.

HAPPY XMAS (WAR IS OVER)

1971 • JOHN & YOKO AND THE PLASTIC ONO BAND WITH THE HARLEM COMMUNITY CHOIR

Songwriters: John Lennon and Yoko Ono
Also covered by: The Fray, Delta Goodrem,
Sarah McLachlan, Alanis Morissette

BY THE TIME the Beatles went their separate ways in 1970, John Lennon and Yoko Ono were already immersed in antiwar activism. The couple recorded "Give Peace a Chance" during their spring 1969 Montreal honeymoon bed-in and celebrated the holidays months later with a pointed message placed on giant billboards in 12 cities: "WAR IS OVER! If You Want It —Happy Christmas from John & Yoko."

In fall 1971, Lennon decided to revisit this slogan, hashing out a simple guitar demo for a song called "Happy Xmas (War Is Over)" at New York City's St. Regis Hotel, where he and Ono were staying. The tune replicated a formula Lennon said worked wonders for 1971's "Imagine," his somber plea for peace that became an unexpected hit: "Put your political message across with a little honey."

Although "Happy Xmas (War Is Over)" does call for an end to violent clashes, the lyrics also sincerely wish everyone around the world a merry Christmas and a happy new year. As a result, the song easily comes across as a warm-and-fuzzy holiday greeting—the kind the Beatles were fond of sharing with fans throughout the '60s. Fittingly, the ever-ambitious Lennon later confessed that he might have also had nonpolitical motives for writing "Happy Xmas (War Is Over)": "I was sick of 'White Christmas.'"

In late October, Lennon and Ono headed to the Record Plant with producer Phil Spector to flesh out the song. Spector was uniquely qualified to work on "Happy Xmas (War Is Over)": Not only had he collaborated with the couple before, most recently on 1971's *Imagine* LP, but he had also produced and orchestrated one of the most famous holiday LPs of all time, *A Christmas Gift for You from Phil Spector*. Spector also reportedly observed that "Happy Xmas (War Is Over)" borrowed elements from a song he had produced, the Paris Sisters' gauzy "I Love How You Love Me."

At any rate, the session featured an impressive lineup of musicians: the great English pianist Nicky Hopkins, who also added wintry percussive sparkle; guitarists Stu Scharf, Chris Osbourne, Teddy Irwin, and Hugh McCracken (the latter fresh off playing on Paul and Linda McCartney's *RAM)*; and legendary drummer Jim Keltner. Together with Lennon and Ono, the group created a song that shimmers like glistening snow, thanks to quivering guitar, lush production, and Lennon's yearning, earnest vocals. Most prominently, Keltner also contributed solemn sleigh bells at the behest of Spector, who had exclaimed, "How can you make a song called 'Happy Christmas' without bells?"

After finishing the basic track, the Harlem Community Choir, made up of 30 talented children, arrived in the studio to add somber harmonies and melodic flourishes. Brilliantly, Lennon lets the choir sing antiwar sentiments while he sticks to singing about good tidings and cheer. In the end, the angelic choir cooing and oohing in the background sounds as if they're conveying a subliminal message of unity and peace—a highly effective way to get a serious point across.

Incredibly enough, "Happy Xmas (War Is Over)"—which was credited upon release to John & Yoko and the Plastic Ono Band with the Harlem Community Choir—didn't chart in the US upon its December 1971 release. The single also didn't surface in the UK until November 1972, although it fared much better on the charts there, peaking at No. 4. Upon Lennon's death in December 1980, "Happy Xmas (War Is Over)" experienced a chart resurgence, reaching a new high of No. 2 in the UK. In the years since, as Lennon and Ono's work together has received more critical acclaim, the song has rightfully become a Christmas staple. In 2022, it even reached the top 40 of the *Billboard* Hot 100 for the first time.

RIVER

1971 • JONI MITCHELL

Songwriter: Joni Mitchell
Also covered by: Tori Amos, Brandi Carlile, Ellie Goulding, Olivia Rodrigo

NOT ALL HOLIDAY SONGS are written to be festive—or even written specifically to be played during the holiday season. That's certainly the case with "River," a center-piece song on *Blue*, the 1971 LP that's often viewed as Joni Mitchell's best work at any time of the year.

"River" has become closely associated with the holiday because of its snowy instrumentation—icy piano and powdery jingle bells—and its setting: The song takes place during a freezing-cold December season and mentions that Christmas is on the way. It also alludes to festive details (for example, chopping down Christmas trees). At the start of "River," Mitchell also taps out a slightly askew, minor-key take on "Jingle Bells" on piano; the reference immediately signals that the song represents a different kind of holiday mood.

Technically, however, "River" isn't a Christmas song. For starters, Mitchell first performed "River" at an October 1970 concert with James Taylor. Moreover, the song also acutely captures the unique pain of going through a breakup during what's supposed to be a blissfully happy time. "We needed a sad Christmas song, didn't we? In the 'bah humbug' of it all?" Mitchell told NPR in 2014 with a laugh, before elaborating on the song's meaning. "Well, it's taking personal responsibility for the failure of a relationship."

This involves plenty of wallowing, of course, with a narrator who blames herself for the breakup and pulls no punches criticizing her own immature behavior. In fact, due to a variety of complicated emotions—embarrassment, grief, shame, relief—the song's protagonist longs to escape her current precarious situation and leave the trappings of the holiday behind. Vocally, Mitchell nails this emotional devastation: She sounds stricken and wistful, owning up to her part in the breakup even if she's not happy but holding space for faint glimmers of optimism. It's clear that her escape could lead to better things—eventually, once the hurt subsides.

According to Mitchell's official website, "River" has been recorded by an eye-popping 918 artists (and counting). That list includes British pop star Ellie Goulding, who hit No. 1 in the UK with a cover in December 2019, as well as Mitchell's folk peer Judy Collins and the pop phenomenon Olivia Rodrigo. Mitchell herself didn't cover the song when she returned to the stage at the 2022 Newport Folk Festival, her first extended live performance since a 2015 brain aneurysm.

However, Mitchell's friend and champion Brandi Carlile—who was by the icon's side at Newport—has tackled "River" as part of full-album performances of *Blue*.

STEP INTO CHRISTMAS

1973 • ELTON JOHN

Songwriters: Elton John (music); Bernie Taupin (lyrics)
Also covered by: The Puppini Sisters, the Wedding Present

WHEN ELTON JOHN headed into the studio to record the stand-alone single "Step into Christmas" in the fall of 1973, he had plenty to celebrate. After becoming a star in the previous few years, thanks to hits such as "Your Song" and "Rocket Man," the pianist earned his first No. 1 single in 1973 with the sassy "Crocodile Rock" and topped the US and UK charts that year with a pair of albums: *Don't Shoot Me I'm Only the Piano Player* and *Goodbye Yellow Brick Road*.

"Step into Christmas" sounds exactly like the kind of song you'd write and perform when you're looking to cap off a banner year that's full of career milestones. Bernie Taupin's lyrics read like an extended, gratitude-filled holiday letter that honors John's stardom; in fact, the song directly says thank you for the previous months. Tellingly, however, "Step into Christmas" invites everyone along for the ride to commemorate the success, watch the snow, and celebrate the holiday with a meal. Christmas is more fun with a crowd, in other words—and John's stardom belongs to everybody.

Both "Step into Christmas" and its somewhat-obscure B-side, "Ho, Ho, Ho (Who'd Be a Turkey at Christmas)," came together on Sunday, November 11,

1973, at London's Morgan Studios. (That was a facility owned by John's sometime-drummer, Barry Morgan.) With John in the studio were his trusty bandmates: guitarist Davey Johnstone, bassist Dee Murray, drummer Nigel Olsson, and percussionist Ray Cooper. Kiki Dee, with whom he'd record the dance classic "Don't Go Breaking My Heart," was also recording at the time and added backing vocals.

According to Elton John's website, "Step into Christmas" was written and recorded in one day. "I came up with this pretty cool acoustic/electric guitar riff and we were off to the races!" Johnstone is quoted as saying. That stair-step riff starts off the song, setting a tone of jubilance, along with a lively bass and John's bar-band boogie piano.

"Step into Christmas" fared well in America, as it topped *Billboard*'s Christmas Singles chart in 1973. Despite some high-profile promotional support—memorably, an über-glam John and his band performed the song on *The Gilbert O'Sullivan Show*—"Step into Christmas" only reached No. 24 on the UK singles charts initially. Over time, however, the song has slowly gained popularity in England and reached the top 10 in 2019.

John wasn't deterred by the initial lukewarm reaction, he told *Melody Maker* in 1973: "The Christmas single is a real loon about and something we'd like to do a lot more of." Sure enough, he has continued to be inspired by "Step into Christmas" throughout the years. In an October 2021 interview on a Dutch radio station, John's good pal Ed Sheeran revealed that he received a call from Elton on Christmas Day about the strong chart showing of "Step into Christmas." According to Sheeran, John exclaimed, "I'm 74 and I'm still having f—ing chart hits. This is great! I want to do another Christmas song. Will you do it with me?" The result of their collaboration was a wildly successful 2021 benefit single, "Merry Christmas," which debuted at No. 1 on the UK charts.

MERRY XMAS EVERYBODY

1973 • SLADE

Songwriters: Noddy Holder and Jim Lea
Also covered by: The Cure, Oasis, Spice Girls, Train

INSPIRATION FOR HOLIDAY songs comes from many places. Just ask glam rockers Slade, whose classic "Merry Xmas Everybody" was inspired by a request from the mother-in-law of bassist/violinist/songwriter Jim Lea. "She said to me, 'Why don't you write a Christmas song, Jim?' I got a bit annoyed," Lea told the *Guardian*. "I was young and full of testosterone and, 'Don't tell me what to do, we're top of the tree.'"

However, Lea not-so-secretly thought it was a good idea and started working on a tune. He recalled that his bandmate, vocalist Noddy Holder, had written a song called "Buy Me a Rocking Chair to Watch the World Go By" in the late 1960s. The rest of Slade wasn't fond of the song at the time—but, several years later, Lea found that bits of the tune fit the Christmas vibe and he framed up a new song based on those bits and shared it with Holder.

The frontman ran with it, he said in a separate interview with the *Guardian*, heading out for a night of drinking at a jazz club to get in a properly festive mood: "I went back to my old bedroom at my mum and dad's, rather merry, and wrote the lyrics in one go." No wonder Holder's words are rather boisterous and cheeky, as the singer muses about what Santa is up to, reminisces about loving family traditions, and asks whether someone is tending to their own personal Christmas wishes. Throughout, the song speaks enthusiastically about the merry times looming during the festive season, and even throws in an oblique, winking reference to the holiday classic "I Saw Mommy Kissing Santa Claus."

Slade recorded "Merry Xmas Everybody" in hot and steamy New York City in August 1973, at the Record Plant, the same place John Lennon recorded his *Mind Games* LP. Fittingly, the band had an absolute blast, Holder told the *Guardian*: "People were going about their business with these four mad Englishmen screaming at the top of our voices about Christmas." Despite the carefree veneer, tracking the song was a bit more of a somber experience, as drummer Don Powell was still on the mend from a very serious car crash that killed his girlfriend and put him in the hospital for weeks on end.

However, the recording environment suited them. Powell could take his time laying down his parts, while both Lea and Holder recalled that Slade recorded vocals outside of the actual studio to get better echo on their singing. The resulting

music is pure Slade swing, with a swaggering glam groove and crunchy riffs, some hypnotic harmonies, and a lilting bridge that feels like a throwback to late-'60s psychedelic pop. Lea especially liked how "Merry Xmas Everybody" turned out. "When I heard the mix, I was chuffed," he told the *Guardian*. "There's not a kid singing or a sleigh bell or anything jingling or jangling. It's just a rock band playing a song."

"Merry Xmas Everybody" was Slade's third No. 1 UK hit of 1973, following "Cum on Feel the Noize" and "Skweeze Me Pleeze Me." The holiday tune spent five weeks at No. 1 on the UK singles chart and was the coveted No. 1

Christmas song of that year. It's proved enduring and lucrative since then, thanks to covers, syncs in movies and commercials, and (re)appearances on the chart.

I WISH IT COULD BE CHRISTMAS EVERYDAY

1973 • WIZZARD

Songwriter: Roy Wood
Also covered by: Cheap Trick, Nick Lowe, Kylie Minogue, Wilson Phillips

WHEN ROY WOOD formed the band Wizzard in 1972, he was already a grizzled music veteran. In the late 1960s, the Birmingham, England, native was the guitarist-vocalist-songwriter for psychedelic rock band the Move. Wood then cofounded the kaleidoscopic orchestral rock troupe Electric Light Orchestra in 1970 alongside Jeff Lynne and Bev Bevan. Wizzard was an offshoot of ELO and ended up staying together for just three years. During this short existence, the band only released two albums but produced one of the biggest glam rock holiday hits: "I Wish It Could Be Christmas Everyday."

As Wood recalled in *Q* magazine in 1996, "I decided to make a Christmas single because they'd been unfashionable for years. We thought it would be worth trying a real rock 'n' roll Christmas song." In the same magazine article, Wizzard saxophonist Mike Burney hinted at where the song's title came from, noting, "I used to say to him, 'Roy, being in this band, it's like Christmas every day.'" Accordingly, the lyrics of "I Wish It Could Be Christmas Everyday" convey just this sentiment:

Life is more vibrant—and carefree—at Christmas. Snow brings grins, not grumbles; music and singing abound; Santa might stay a spell if he's invited. Oh, and if your beard is frozen by the cold? No problem—just take a nap by the fire and warm up.

The notoriously perfectionist Wood went all-out to make "I Wish It Could Be Christmas Everyday" sound unique. He recorded a basic musical track comprising acoustic guitar and cowbell, and then onto this foundation piled various textures and sounds. That included a jumble of percussion instruments, chilly sleigh bells, and unexpected found sounds—for example, the jingling of a metal cash register opens the song.

To record his vocal part, Wood got in a festive mood by decking out the studio in holiday decorations and bringing in huge fans to make the room colder. As the pièce de résistance, a choir of kids from Birmingham's Stockland Green School visited the studio one day and sang their hearts out. The result is the kind of song that feels like it takes place in a pretty snow globe. Wood belts out the lyrics like a parade ringleader as the beautiful musical cacophony cascades around him like fluffy flakes.

"People talk about it being over-produced, but the effect I was trying to get was something I personally associate with Christmas, that Walt Disney music feel," Wood said to *Q*. "It's Disney movie music without the film."

Wizzard had nabbed two straight No. 1 hits in the UK prior to the release of "I Wish It Could Be Christmas Everyday" and Wood himself hoped to earn the UK's coveted Christmas No. 1 song position. Alas, the tune ended up reaching No. 4 on the UK singles chart upon release, kept from the top of the charts by another seminal glam rock holiday tune, Slade's "Merry Xmas Everybody" (see page 93).

To date, that was the chart high point for "I Wish It Could Be Christmas Everyday," although Wood pushed for more success several times. He rerecorded the song in 1981, but it didn't reach the top 40; a subsequent reissue of that version with an extended 12-inch take only reached No. 23. However, Wood can take comfort in the fact that every holiday season since 2007, the original version of the song reenters the singles chart. The hopeful promise of "I Wish It Could Be Christmas Everyday" ended up coming true.

THE SNOW MISER SONG
& THE HEAT MISER SONG

1974 • SNOW MISER & HEAT MISER

Songwriter: Jules Bass (lyrics); Maury Laws (music)
Also covered by: Big Bad Voodoo Daddy ("Heat Miser"),
45 Grave ("Snow Miser")

BY 1974, creative icons Arthur Rankin Jr. and Jules Bass—the cofounders of Rankin/
Bass Productions—were holiday TV special royalty. A decade before, the company's innovative stop-motion animation style brought the beloved Christmas song
"Rudolph, the Red-Nosed Reindeer" to life. Following the success of that special came
adaptations based on songs like "The Little Drummer Boy" and "Frosty the Snowman,"
as well as animated interpretations of books like author Phyllis McGinley's children's
tale *The Year Without a Santa Claus*.

Newly commissioned musical pieces were always an integral part of Rankin/
Bass TV specials. And for the TV special *The Year Without a Santa Claus*, these
came in the form of a matched set of strutting big band numbers: "The Snow Miser
Song" and "The Heat Miser Song," the theme songs for a pair of weather opposites.
As their names imply, Snow Miser loves things cold, while Heat Miser digs high
temperatures. Rankin/Bass music director Maury Laws composed the music, while
Jules Bass wrote the lyrics.

The differentiators of each song were the voice-over artists. On *The Year
Without a Santa Claus*, Dick Shawn—an actor who costarred in 1963's *It's a Mad
Mad Mad Mad World*—sang "The Snow Miser Song," while veteran TV actor George
S. Irving handled "The Heat Miser Song." Both bring a lovably cranky-goofy vibe

to the characters, although Shawn's chilly portrayal is a bit more over the top than Irving's more regal take. (Perhaps understandable—after all, winter is the Snow Miser's time to shine!)

Both songs have endured in pop culture, although one of the more endearing takes took place when Arnold Schwarzenegger, as Mr. Freeze, watches *The Year Without a Santa Claus* (and, by extension, listens to "The Snow Miser Song") in 1997's *Batman and Robin*. Schwarzenegger is beyond enthusiastic about the tune and even waves his arms like an orchestra conductor while encouraging his minions to sing along to "The Snow Miser Song." A 2006 film version of the animated special also boasted some miserly star power, as comedic icon Michael McKean portrayed Snow Miser and Harvey Fierstein played Heat Miser. Fierstein is mischievous and slightly evil, in contrast to the cooler McKean, who resembles an aging rock star who's (appropriately) cool as a cucumber.

OUR WORLD/BROTHERS

1977 • EMMET OTTER'S JUG-BAND CHRISTMAS

Songwriter: Paul Williams
Also covered by: My Morning Jacket

THE VISIONARY PUPPETEER Jim Henson was responsible for directing some of the most memorable Christmas specials of all time. Among them was 1977's *Emmet Otter's Jug-Band Christmas*. Based on a 1971 book by beloved children's authors Russell and Lillian Hoban, the TV special follows the plight of gentle Emmet, who strives to earn money to buy his beloved Ma, Alice, a nice Christmas present. Emmet's solution is to form a ragtag jug band and attempt to capture the $50 first prize at a talent show.

The fictional band performed some very real, heartfelt songs with lyrics penned by a decorated songwriter named Paul Williams. Prior to working on *Emmet Otter's Jug-Band Christmas*, Williams won a Grammy and an Oscar for the lyrics of *A Star Is Born*'s "Evergreen," a song composed and sung by Barbra Streisand. His songs were also recorded by the Carpenters ("Rainy Days and Mondays," "We've Only Just Begun") and he'd later find additional success thanks to *The Muppet Movie*, as he co-wrote "Rainbow Connection."

However, Williams's music for *Emmet Otter's Jug-Band Christmas* represented his first collaboration with Henson. The songwriter imbued his work for the puppets with humanity, an approach also espoused by Henson. "I think of them as otters and porcupines," Williams told *American Theatre* in 2021. "I don't think of them as some object at the end of somebody's arm. There's such an absolute, distinct personality."

Sung as a call-and-response duet between Ma (Alice) Otter and Emmet's jug band, the poignant "Our World/Brothers" (also known as "Brothers in Our World") overflows with personality. That's largely due to actress Marilyn Sokol, who voices Alice with tremendous grace. Her soprano singing voice is regal and proud, a perfect foil for the band's humble harmonies. Subtle, folksy instrumental accompaniment—a droning organ, buckling string instruments, a kazoo—adds color, although the singing is clearly the centerpiece.

As its name implies, "Our World/Brothers" is technically a mash-up of two songs, "Brothers" and "Our World." It's a particularly lovely combination because the lyrics reinforce several of the TV special's messages: Even if people seem different on the surface, they have more in common than they think—and keeping your mind *and* heart open to new ideas leads to an abundance of love and friendship. In no small part because of this sweet theme, "Our World/Brothers" ended up a highlight of the *Emmet Otter's Jug-Band Christmas* soundtrack, which has become a holiday season staple alongside the TV special.

FATHER CHRISTMAS

1977 • THE KINKS

Songwriter: Ray Davies
Also covered by: Bad Religion, Cheap Trick, OK Go, Smash Mouth

NOT ALL CHRISTMAS SONGS focus exclusively on the holidays. Much as "White Christmas" obliquely referenced the somber political climate during World War II, and Stevie Wonder's "Someday at Christmas" reflected the social changes of the late 1960s, the Kinks' scrappy "Father Christmas" is a biting commentary on class differences and the economic hardships facing England in the late 1970s.

The song's protagonist is a department store Santa who is threatened and robbed by a group of tough kids. The hooligans tell Santa he can deliver toys to more well-off families. Instead, the kids demand money—and, more selflessly, ask Santa to get their fathers a job. Pointedly, "Father Christmas" also includes a verse in which an omniscient narrator reminds listeners to keep the less fortunate in mind while celebrating.

Believe it or not, the *Guardian* reported in 1977 that UK radio stations were reluctant to play "Father Christmas." Admittedly, that could've been because the Kinks were in a fallow commercial period at the time. After enjoying immense success in the 1960s as part of the British Invasion, the band veered off into more experimental territory in the 1970s. (In a reversal, however, the band's 1977 LP *Sleepwalker* was their highest-charting US album to date, beating even their well-regarded earlier work.)

Kinks cofounder Ray Davies, who wrote and produced "Father Christmas," theorized that the song's weighty message may have deterred the powers that be at UK radio, especially because the commentary was coming from a veteran band like the Kinks. "It seems all right for the new wave bands to say something," Davies told the *Guardian* in 1977, "but if you've been around you get pounced on."

Recorded at the Kinks' London studio, Konk Studios, and polished in October 1977, "Father Christmas" is hardly a stodgy song from an over-the-hill band. In fact, the music bristles with punk energy and attitude. After starting off in a deceptively straightforward way with brisk jingle bells and piano, the tune explodes into a raucous guitar song that hews closer to the roughshod rock favored by cutting-edge artists like Elvis Costello and Nick Lowe.

The Kinks performed "Father Christmas" on their late 1977 US tour and also performed two special Christmas shows that year at the Rainbow Theatre in London. The Christmas Eve show was broadcast live as an Old Grey Whistle Test Special and featured an appropriately spirited "Father Christmas." Ray Davies stormed onstage in full Santa regalia—beard, sack of presents, and all—and tossed trinkets into the crowd—before he and the Kinks launched into a freewheeling version of the song.

Despite this high-profile airing, "Father Christmas" didn't make a dent on the charts in the US or the UK. However, it has since become a rock 'n' roll holiday classic. Ray's brother, Kinks cofounder Dave Davies, even keeps the song alive on his own. "It was a lot of fun," he told ABC Radio in 2018, about recording the song. "I even do it in my own [solo] set sometimes. It's a very funny song."

JESUS CHRIST

1978 • BIG STAR

Songwriter: Alex Chilton
Also covered by: The Decemberists, Kristin Hersh,
Mike Mills (R.E.M.), the Monkees

IT'S SAID THAT the über-cool '60s band the Velvet Underground didn't make a huge splash with their debut album—but the people who did hear the LP decided to start a band. You might say a similar thing about the cult power-pop act Big Star. Formed in Memphis, Tennessee, in 1971, the quartet crafted exquisite pop music that spoke to the agonies and ecstasies of being a human navigating an often-heartbreaking world.

Big Star never made much of a commercial dent during its original existence, but the group's music resonated with the ears that mattered. "When I heard Big Star, I recognized people who did what I wanted to do," R.E.M. bassist Mike Mills told *Garden & Gun* in 2022. "They wrote songs that both rocked and were sensitive and beautiful, sometimes at the same time. It was an encapsulation of everything I believed a band should be."

Over the years, Mills has often performed Big Star's "Jesus Christ" in concert, including with a group of musicians who tour and honor the group's music. The song is certainly about Christmas—the chorus plainly and directly mentions the birth of Jesus, and the lyrics reference imagery found in existing hymns. However, "Jesus Christ" is less about the universal experience of the holiday and more about how the event ripples out and prompts personal reflection and rebirth.

The album on which "Jesus Christ" appeared was released several years after the members of Big Star went their separate ways. To make things even more complex, in the UK the LP was known as *The Third Album*, but in the US it was called *3rd*. (Adding to the confusion, the record was later issued on CD as *Third/Sister Lovers*.) While this full-length album contains some of Big Star's most challenging songwriting, "Jesus Christ" itself is one of the sweetest-sounding songs in the group's catalog.

After starting with a 20-second instrumental intro of avant-garde improvisation that's somewhere between jazz and bossa nova, the tune blooms into a gorgeous, soul-kissed song with chiming guitar riffs and Alex Chilton's weathered (if earnest) vocals. The details stitched into "Jesus Christ" elevate the song: a thundering timpani, an echoing saxophone solo on the bridge, and easygoing grooves. It's a joyful holiday song filtered through Big Star's fractured pop lens, meaning it's something special.

PLEASE COME HOME FOR CHRISTMAS

1978 • EAGLES

Songwriter: Charles Brown
Also covered by: Jon Bon Jovi, Willie Nelson, Darius Rucker

THE EAGLES' 1976 album *Hotel California* was one of the biggest albums of the 1970s, owing to the epic title track and songs such as "Life in the Fast Lane." So how did the California band decide to follow up this blockbuster? By releasing a one-off single: an understated, soulful version of the 1960 R&B hit "Please Come Home for Christmas," backed by a B-side called "Funky New Year."

Driven by understated piano played by Glenn Frey and equally subtle guitars from Joe Walsh and Don Felder—adding up to a gentle, waltzing tempo—the song is faithful to the bluesy original. Notably, "Please Come Home for Christmas" was also the first time Timothy B. Schmit contributed bass to an Eagles song; his parts add subtle verve that enhance the vibe.

In addition to keeping a steady 6/8-time signature groove, vocalist-drummer Don Henley captures the ache of the lyrics in a smoky voice that's infused with sorrow and melancholy. Although relatives are sharing good tidings, and Christmas music is in the air, the narrator laments that they feel quite alone, in large part because their love is far away for the holidays. The only thing that can ease their pain is to have their beloved return home—a scenario that seems completely unlikely.

Charles Brown, who was one of Christmas music's most underrated musicians and songwriters, wrote "Please Come Home for Christmas." He cut his teeth first as the pianist-vocalist for Johnny Moore's Three Blazers—which had hits in the late 1940s with "Drifting Blues" and the soon-to-be-holiday-classic "Merry Christmas Baby"—and then as leader of the Charles Brown Trio, which nabbed a major R&B hit in 1949 with "Trouble Blues." In the late 1950s, Brown ended up in the Cincinnati, Ohio, area as the music director for Frank "Screw" Andrews.

Andrews, described in a 1990 *Cincinnati Post* article as a "racketeer," reportedly took care of Brown's expenses, paying the musician $750 a week and covering his rent and a car. In turn, Brown performed and booked artists at a Newport, Kentucky, club called the Golden Lounge.

This musical activity caught the ear of Syd Nathan, head of the Cincinnati label King Records, known for being a legendary force in funk and R&B. In 1960, King issued a seven-inch single of a new Charles Brown composition, "Please Come Home for Christmas." The single was co-credited to Gene Redd, an A&R employee at King Records. This irked Brown, he told the *Cincinnati Post* in 1990: "I hadn't copyrighted it, so they put a copyright on it and put Gene Redd's name on it and he didn't have anything to do with it."

It's easy to understand why Brown would be upset, as "Please Come Home for Christmas" struck a particularly emotional chord. In the December 31, 1960 *Billboard* issue, the single was named an R&B Best Buy, and it eventually became a holiday classic, reaching No. 1 on the Christmas Singles chart in 1972. Decades later, the Eagles, too, had success with the song. It reached No. 18 on the *Billboard* Hot 100 in early 1979 and returned to No. 40 in 2021, the band's first top 40 hit since 1994.

CHRISTMAS RAPPIN'

1979 • KURTIS BLOW

Songwriters: Kurtis Blow, Robert "Rocky" Ford Jr.,
Denzil Miller, J.B. Moore, Larry Smith

MAINSTREAM MUSIC experienced seismic changes in the late 1970s and into the early 1980s, as new sounds and styles began to appear on the radio and in the charts: synth-pop, power-pop, punk, new wave, and hip-hop. Christmas music embraced these shifts, as the young artists within these genres put their own stamp on tradition.

Next to the Sugarhill Gang, which had a hit with "Rapper's Delight" in late 1979 and into 1980, one of the most influential figures in hip-hop's mainstream rise was Kurtis Blow. Born Kurtis Walker and raised in Harlem, he was the first rapper signed to a major record label, after he inked a deal with Mercury Records in 1979. The reason he was signed? His holiday original, "Christmas Rappin'."

The genesis of the Christmas song came from two *Billboard* writers, Robert "Rocky" Ford Jr. and J.B. Moore. A *Smithsonian* article written by renowned hip-hop scholar Bill Adler, who was once the publicist at Def Jam Records during the 1980s, noted that Ford's girlfriend became pregnant. With journalism feeling precarious, Ford was looking for a solid revenue stream to support his growing family and landed on the perfect idea: a Christmas song—specifically a hip-hop Christmas song. Moore was also inspired by the notion and reportedly left a bunch of lyrics for a proposed tune on Ford's answering machine.

However, the song needed the proper voice. Although several artists were in contention for a collaboration, Kurtis Blow came on the pair's radar thanks to future hip-hop impresario Russell Simmons. Simmons tipped Ford off to a summer 1979 live performance by Blow, and the latter's talent and charismatic presence sealed the deal. Next, Blow and the songwriters linked up with musicians Denzil Miller and Larry Smith to work up the musical side. "My style of music was in between Chic, progressive disco funk, and James Brown, so that was the style of 'Christmas Rappin'," Blow told *Hip-Hop Evolution*. Musically, that translated to strutting guitar, bouncy bass, and delightful flourishes like tinkling piano and stuttering rhythm breaks.

Blow also helped hone the song's lyrics, building on the existing thematic foundation and injecting his own personality into the song. "J.B. Moore wrote the first half of that song—all the parts about Christmas—but I wrote the second half with all the party references," Blow told the website Rock the Bells, noting that he was inspired by fellow local hip-hop influencers DJ Hollywood and Eddie Cheeba.

After starting with some recited lines from "'Twas the Night Before Christmas," the song tells the tale of a wild and wonderful holiday party that's visited by Santa Claus himself. Rather than shy away from the shindig, Saint Nick joins in the revelry before delivering some wonderful gifts. However, "Christmas Rappin'" imparts some important wisdom near the end: Telling your friends you love and care for them is the best, most priceless gift of all. Throughout, Blow's delivery is expressive and even creates suspense: He sounds as if he's telling his own Christmas bedtime story.

"Christmas Rappin'" was completed well before the holiday season but wasn't a surefire hit. In fact, more than 20 labels turned down the single before Mercury Records took a chance on signing Blow. The gamble paid off: "Christmas Rappin'" sold very well—estimates in interviews fall somewhere between 350,000 and 370,000 copies—setting the stage for Blow's subsequent breakthrough chart hit, the 12-inch single of 1980's "The Breaks," which was certified gold for 500,000 records sold. All this success allowed Blow to record a full-length album, another milestone in rap and hip-hop's evolution. And "Christmas Rappin'" itself also transcended its holiday association thanks to samples in tunes such as Next's "Too Close" and the Beastie Boys' "Hold It Now, Hit It."

DECEMBER WILL BE MAGIC AGAIN

1979 • KATE BUSH

Songwriter: Kate Bush

DECADES BEFORE *Stranger Things'* use of "Running Up That Hill (A Deal with God)" made Kate Bush a household name, she was something of a TV star herself. Her performances on high-profile TV shows were legendary for their thoughtful presentations, while her music videos were artistic and full of intricate choreography. For example, in a clip for her 1978 debut single, "Wuthering Heights," she dances gracefully in a grassy field wearing a billowing red dress. Fans later embraced the iconic music video, launching annual gatherings where they celebrated

"The Most Wuthering Heights Day Ever" by donning their own red dresses and frolicking in a field.

In 1979, Bush entered holiday infamy with a Christmas-themed TV special titled, simply, *Kate*. Not only does the music-heavy special boast multiple guest appearances by Peter Gabriel, it also features Bush performing a new Christmas song, "December Will Be Magic Again." Tucked away at the piano, she trills about the magic of the season—Santa rising up the chimney, Bing Crosby's "White Christmas," snow-covered scenes, mistletoe—and how these details add joy and twinkles. As is her way, she drops a literary reference (Oscar Wilde) and delivers these lyrics in an operatic warble with delicate sparkle.

Bush recorded a studio version of the song at Abbey Road Studios Studio Two on November 23, 1979. With her were two frequent collaborators, guitarist Alan Murphy and drummer/percussionist Preston Heyman, as well as bassist Kuma Harada. Several years ago, Abbey Road dug up the original recording sheets, which listed the session as running from mid-afternoon to well into the night.

The same week *Kate* premiered, Bush appeared on the BBC's *Christmas Snowtime Special*, performing a slightly different version of "December Will Be Magic Again." Most notably, this take features prominent, slinky congas played by Heyman, as well as acrobatic vocal melodies and a lilting slide whistle. Bush also eschewed the piano, preferring instead to do interpretive dancing and glitter-spreading while seated in a plush red chair.

A congas-less version of "December Will Be Magic Again" was released as a single in 1980 and, curiously enough, didn't come with a music video. The single also only charted at No. 29 in the UK—a surprisingly low showing, considering that she had three top 20 singles in 1980—although it nearly reached the top 10 in Ireland. However, the different versions of "December Will Be Magic Again" have popped up on holiday music compilations. With the rise of video-streaming platforms, both Bush's visual aesthetic and holiday special have become inspirational beacons for younger generations.

WHEN THE RIVER MEETS THE SEA

1979 • JOHN DENVER AND THE MUPPETS

Songwriter: Paul Williams

THE FLOPPY, FURRY MUPPETS were pop culture dynamos in the late 1970s. Not only did they dominate TV with a clever variety show, dubbed *The Muppet Show*, but they became movie stars thanks to the 1979 film *The Muppet Movie*. That same year, the Muppets teamed up with bespectacled folk singer John Denver—one of the most popular soft rock/folk singers of the 1970s—for a TV special, *John Denver and the Muppets: A Christmas Together*. In a case of art imitating life, the special finds Denver and the motley Muppets crew working through mirth and mayhem to put together a Christmas special.

An LP released in conjunction with the TV special, *John Denver and the Muppets: A Christmas Together*, made a modest showing on both the country and pop albums charts and was certified platinum in early 1980. According to Henson archives, recording for the album began in June 1979, months before the crew recorded the TV show. The LP boasted some star power in addition to the credited musicians: Former Byrds member Herb Pedersen contributed arrangements as well as banjo and guitars, while several legendary session players who were part of the Wrecking Crew—including flutist and saxophonist Jim Horn and drummer Hal Blaine—also played on the record.

One of the LP's most touching moments came when Denver and Kermit the Frog's nephew, Robin, sing "When the River Meets the Sea." Musically, it's a pastoral tune that starts off with just Robin (voiced by puppeteer Jerry Nelson) singing while accompanied by simple keyboards. When Denver joins the fray, the song blooms to include flute, acoustic and electric guitars, and strings, as well as robust backing vocals. Robin and Denver are perfect vocal foils; the former resembles Willie Nelson, while the latter is majestic and regal-sounding, giving the material proper gravitas.

Songwriter Paul Williams originally wrote the song for Jim Henson's *Emmet Otter's Jug-Band Christmas*. In fact, "When the River Meets the Sea" appeared in the TV special, sung by Emmet Otter and his mother, Alice, as they remember their departed family patriarch, Pa. Accordingly, the song's lyrics don't reference Christmas or the holidays; in fact, the song is much more about birth and death and the way we accumulate knowledge, thanks to the circle of life. It's both melancholy and comforting, as the song posits that as we near the end of our days, we'll glean valuable wisdom that'll let us leave the Earth peacefully.

"When the River Meets the Sea" has also transcended its association with Christmas; in fact, Jerry Nelson—who was known for multiple Sesame Street characters in addition to Robin the Frog, including Count von Count—and puppeteer Louise Gold performed a moving, hymn-like version of the song at Jim Henson's 1990 memorial service. Much later, Jimmy Fallon enlisted both Robin and Kermit for a rendition of the song on his late-night talk show. Denver and the Muppets, meanwhile, would team up again a few times, including on a 1982 holiday special and album, *Rocky Mountain Holiday*.

GRANDMA GOT OVER BY A REINDEER

1979 • ELMO & PATSY

Songwriter: Randy Brooks
Also covered by: The Irish Rovers, Cledus T. Judd, Less Than Jake

DURING THE 1960s and 1970s, country artists such as Johnny Cash, Loretta Lynn, and Tompall Glaser covered songs penned by the writer Shel Silverstein. Silverstein's work was often whimsical, if occasionally macabre, much like his renowned poetry books, such as *Where the Sidewalk Ends*. This silly-but-dark spirit also permeates the deceptively rollicking "Grandma Got Run Over by a Reindeer." Penned by a Texas musician named Randy Brooks and recorded by the musical duo Elmo & Patsy, the tune tells the sad tale of a grandma who overindulges on eggnog and is trampled by Santa and his reindeer crew.

The tune certainly has a wicked sense of humor—the lyrics note that a sleigh-driving man who cavorts with elves shouldn't have a license—and mentions that the entire family is grieving; Grandpa is recovering by watching football and playing cards, while other relatives are wondering if they should return gifts. (The consensus is yes.) However, "Grandma Got Run Over by a Reindeer" has a very prominent silver lining that's anything but a bummer—the accident makes the narrator and his grandpa believe in Santa Claus.

Brooks wrote "Grandma Got Run Over by a Reindeer" in 1977, inspired by two things: his wig-wearing grandmother, who occasionally overdid it on the spirits, and a Merle Haggard song. "I went to bed with a notebook and finished the song in the shower the next day," he told the *Dallas Morning News* in 1996. Brooks performed it live for the next few years with his band, Young Country, both locally and out of town. In fact, he first crossed paths with Elmo & Patsy in Lake Tahoe: The brakes on Young Country's van froze up, causing the band to stay put long enough to meet the duo.

Elmo & Patsy was the recording moniker of California married couple Elmo and Patsy Shropshire, who had unusual backgrounds: Before getting into music, he was a veterinarian, and she was a flight attendant. The duo had released three albums prior to "Grandma Got Run Over by a Reindeer," including two under the name the Homestead Act, and were a well-honed live group. When Elmo heard Brooks's composition, he was bowled over. After adding it to their set, Elmo & Patsy told UPI that the song became a popular concert request, especially with grandmas: "We'd play it three times a night in the middle of July."

Buoyed by the response, the couple shelled out $2,000 to press 600 copies of the "Grandma Got Run Over by a Reindeer" single. Musically, the studio version of the song boasts a country-folk approach, infused by the duo's bluegrass background. Elmo's rough-and-tumble twang brings an easygoing vibe to the song, which is rather cheerful despite the subject matter; at one point, the duo even interpolates "Jingle Bells."

While the self-released single didn't connect with audiences or record labels initially, "Grandma Got Run Over by a Reindeer" soon became a regional hit in the San Francisco Bay area after a radio DJ named Gene Nelson supported the single. At the time, plans called for wider distribution, at the nice price of just 98 cents per single. In the meantime, it flew off the shelves locally: The *Oakland Tribune* reported that Elmo & Patsy sold 200 copies to the Tower Records store at Fisherman's Wharf in 1979—and received *another* order for that many copies just two days later.

It took a few years, but "Grandma Got Run Over by a Reindeer" did indeed take off nationally. Elmo & Patsy rerecorded and reissued the song in 1982, and this version exploded after being issued once again by Epic Records in 1984. It reached No. 1 on *Billboard*'s Christmas Hits chart, beating out Bing Crosby's perennial "White Christmas," and was also named the Society of European Stage Authors and Composers (SESAC)'s country song of the year. In subsequent years, Elmo cut solo versions—he and Patsy had divorced in 1985—and rerecorded the tune again himself under the name Dr. Elmo. Patsy, meanwhile, has also performed the tune as a solo act. A 2000 animated Christmas TV special based on the song also ensured that its legacy lives on for future generations of wicked Christmas consumers.

WONDERFUL CHRISTMASTIME

1979 • PAUL McCARTNEY

Songwriter: Paul McCartney
Also covered by: Demi Lovato, Kylie Minogue, the Monkees, Diana Ross

CHRISTMAS SONGS generally don't cause controversy. One major exception, however, is "Wonderful Christmastime." Despite being written and performed by Paul McCartney—who's inarguably one of the most famous and respected musicians of all time because he was a *member of the Beatles*—the synth-driven song is incredibly polarizing. People either seem to love "Wonderful Christmastime" or loathe it; they're rarely indifferent to the song.

It's difficult to see why "Wonderful Christmastime" causes such a strong reaction. McCartney was an especially sentimental lyricist in the 1970s, and "Wonderful Christmastime" expresses genuine delight at the festive season while encouraging people to enjoy the present moment. A lively children's choir trills a happy song. Other people are in a good mood because they're at a party celebrating the holidays. Nobody wants to be anywhere else; nobody wishes the night were going differently. The spirit of Christmas abounds.

"Wonderful Christmastime" emerged in November 1979 during a transitional time for McCartney. His post-Beatles band Wings was disintegrating after a final studio album (1979's *Back to the Egg*) and one last UK tour. McCartney was simultaneously rekindling his solo career. In fact, he tracked "Wonderful Christmastime" during the summer of 1979 at his studios in Sussex, England, and Scotland, as part of the sessions for 1980's *McCartney II.* That solo LP emerged from endless experimentation—in fact, McCartney played every single instrument on the album—and contained forays into synthesizer-based music, notably the blippy "Temporary Secretary."

Perhaps unsurprisingly, "Wonderful Christmastime" feels like a bridge between his work with Wings and these new solo tunes. (Also, fittingly, the song has appeared as a bonus track on reissues of both *Back to the Egg* and *McCartney II.*) An echoing synthesizer melody dominates, circulating like zaps of electricity around more traditional sleigh bells and blocky vocal harmonies. In hindsight, "Wonderful Christmastime" feels like an avant-garde electronic music composition.

"Wonderful Christmastime" was a big success in the UK, reaching No. 6 on the singles charts—McCartney's highest-charting hit since Wings' 1974 manifesto "Band on the Run"—and setting the stage for McCartney's early '80s commercial renaissance. However, Wings did perform "Wonderful Christmastime" on their swan song tour, playing up the song's vibe by having fake snow fall during the set. The band also appeared in the song's music video. Directed by Russell Mulcahy—who would find fame in the '80s as the director of elaborate videos for Ultravox, Elton John, Duran Duran, and others—the clip boasts an upbeat mood that was at odds with actual relations within the band.

By contrast, "Wonderful Christmastime" barely dented the chart in the US in 1979. Over time, however, "Wonderful Christmastime" has become a holiday tradition, reaching No. 28 on the *Billboard* Hot 100 in early 2021. McCartney also periodically performs the tune live during solo shows, and has collaborated on new versions of "Wonderful Christmastime" with Straight No Chaser and the Roots and Jimmy Fallon. And despite the grouchy feelings many have toward the song, it's been very good for McCartney's bank account: In 2010, *Forbes* estimated that the song earned him between $400,000 and $600,000 per year.

CHRISTMAS IS THE TIME TO SAY 'I LOVE YOU'

1981 · BILLY SQUIER

Songwriter: Billy Squier
Also covered by: Darlene Love, Katharine McPhee, SR-71

IN THE EARLY 1980s, you'd have been hard-pressed to find a bigger rock star than Billy Squier. The Massachusetts-born multi-instrumentalist cut his teeth in several hip Boston bands in the 1970s before going solo and breaking out with the 1981 LP *Don't Say No*. That album contained multiple rock radio hits—including "Lonely Is the Night," "The Stroke," and "In the Dark"—and led Squier to open shows for arena rock royalty, including Foreigner, Journey, and REO Speedwagon.

However, Squier wasn't content to just dominate the airwaves with larger-than-life original tunes about isolation, loneliness, and music industry critiques. The flip side of his 1981 single "My Kinda Lover" was an exuberant holiday song called "Christmas Is the Time to Say 'I Love You.'" Squier, his band, and a group of pals recorded the song in August 1981 at the Power Station in New York City. According to the magazine *Cash Box*, this motley crew included King Crimson cofounder Robert Fripp, Meat Loaf collaborator Karla DeVito, Sweet's Steve Priest, and the Knack's Doug Fieger.

The magazine slyly notes that this group were "feted with a Christmas-style turkey dinner (and spirits)" to "create the appropriate atmosphere of good cheer." Mission accomplished: "Christmas Is the Time to Say 'I Love You'" starts with the revelers lustily singing along to the chorus, and later incorporates plenty of background hoots and hollers for good measure. The song's instrumentation matched this revelry. A modern spin on '50s rock 'n' roll, the tune incorporates freewheeling bar-band piano, a loose and bluesy guitar solo, and Squier singing earnest lyrics that encourage people to express affection and gratitude to friends and loved ones. All told, the song perfectly captures how the holidays bring people together in mirth, celebration, and *maybe* even overindulging.

"Christmas Is the Time to Say 'I Love You'" received rock radio airplay in 1981 and an official single release in 1983; the latter's B-side was a decidedly unserious kazoo version of "White Christmas." (Unsurprisingly, that song also dated from the raucous Power Station sessions.) Despite Squier's previous success, the tune didn't chart—although, in a nod to the changing times, he filmed a music video for the song in 1981 for MTV. The gesture doubled as a thank-you note to the just-launched 24/7 music video cable channel. Squier was one of the first major artists to receive a career boost from MTV, as his videos were in regular rotation.

For the "Christmas Is the Time to Say 'I Love You'" video clip, Squier re-created the upbeat studio vibe, singing the tune in front of a joyful chorus comprising MTV staff and radio personalities. One of the five original MTV video hosts, Martha Quinn, even told Yahoo! in 2016, "If I had to go back in time and revisit one day, like if I could get into the DeLorean and go back to one moment, it [would] probably be this."

CHRISTMAS WRAPPING

1981 • THE WAITRESSES

Songwriter: Chris Butler
Also covered by: The Donnas, Kylie Minogue (with Iggy Pop),
Save Ferris, the Spice Girls

THE HOLIDAY SEASON isn't always sugarplum fairies and neatly wrapped gifts. After preparing for parties or stressful family visits, sometimes you're just not in the mood to be merry or make nice. Luckily, the Waitresses have just the song for Christmas cranks: the exasperated "Christmas Wrapping," which features a protagonist relieved to be spending Christmas alone after a hectic year.

However, "Christmas Wrapping" isn't *really* about a holiday grinch. Read the lyrics closely and you'll discover that the song actually revolves around a chance meet-cute. The narrator and a man she met at a ski shop have tried to meet up all year but were thwarted at every turn by obstacles: bad weather, schedule misalignment, a dead car, sunburn. On Christmas, however, the fairy tale concludes in the best way possible: She runs into the same man at the store because they both forgot to buy cranberries. Cue a happy ending—and a happy holiday.

Waitresses founder Chris Butler wrote "Christmas Wrapping" due to pressure from Michael Zilkha, cofounder of the Waitresses' label, the experimental-leaning ZE Records. Zilkha was plotting out a holiday album, a bewildered Butler told the *Guardian*: "You have Alan Vega and Lydia Lunch on your label—not festive nonsense! I hoped they would forget the idea, but they didn't." Zilkha was indeed undeterred; in fact, he was so determined to have the Waitresses aboard that he preemptively booked the band studio time at the legendary Electric Lady Studios.

Being festive on command isn't always easy, but Butler and the rest of the Waitresses spent a few weeks working up a tune and then took another few days to record the song. (Yes, Butler clarified years later, the title is a nod to Kurtis Blow's 1979 smash "Christmas Rappin'.") The tune begins with sleigh bells that conjure "Jingle Bells" and then incorporates shuffling grooves and a slippery guitar riff that echo both '50s rock 'n' roll and punkish new wave. Vocalist Patty Donahue speak-sings over the rollicking music in her usual nonchalant way. However, she also adds the right amount of deadpan humor to the irreverent proceedings, such as when she utters a mild expletive to punctuate the lyric about forgetting cranberries.

It helped that the Waitresses' lineup at the time included New York musical royalty (ex-Television drummer Billy Ficca) as well as top-notch instrumentalists: future B-52s bassist Tracy Wormworth, avant-garde saxophonist Mars Williams, and guest trumpeter Dave Buck. Williams and Buck especially add color, contributing enthusiastic playing that mirrors the melody; Williams played both alto and tenor sax, and Buck also later improvised some raucous freestyle parts. Wormworth, meanwhile, told the *Guardian* that she was inspired by the iconic bassline of Chic's dance-floor-unifier "Good Times": "I wasn't trying to rip it off, but I was heavily inspired by it. I sat in the studio and worked out note for note what I would play."

Despite the hurried genesis, Butler told Yahoo! it "was a very good recording experience. But we fulfilled our obligation and went back on the road—and kind of forgot about it." As it turned out, the song ended up being unforgettable. "Christmas Wrapping" was a marquee part of the ZE Records holiday LP, *A Christmas Record*, which was released in 1981. During the 1982 holiday season, the song also appeared on the Waitresses' *I Could Rule the World If I Could Only Get the Parts* EP and started receiving heavy US rock radio airplay. (Trade ads at the time played up the song's title, posing pun-heavy questions related to wrapping presents.) In the UK, "Christmas Wrapping" landed at No. 45 on the singles chart.

PEACE ON EARTH/ LITTLE DRUMMER BOY

1982 • DAVID BOWIE & BING CROSBY

Songwriters: Katherine Kennicott Davis, Henry Onorati, Harry Simeone ("Little Drummer Boy"); Ian Fraser, Larry Grossman, Alan Kohan ("Peace on Earth")

IN LATE SUMMER 1977, it was difficult to find a more head-scratching pairing than David Bowie and Bing Crosby. At the time, Bowie was youth culture personified—an artsy rock 'n' roll chameleon in the middle of releasing a series of dark and experimental albums that would become known as the Berlin Trilogy, so named because he recorded them in Germany with cutting-edge collaborators such as synth wizard Brian Eno.

Crosby, meanwhile, was decidedly of an older generation—a crooner in the twilight of his career who favored standards and more traditional music, and who had just started touring again after some health issues. And while his holiday music pedigree was secure thanks to "White Christmas," Crosby certainly seemed like an unlikely candidate for a Bowie duet, much less a Bowie duet meant for a holiday special.

Nevertheless, on September 11, 1977, the duo found themselves at ATV Elstree Studios filming a segment for Crosby's upcoming *Bing Crosby's Merrie Olde Christmas* TV special. Not only did Bing introduce an airing of Bowie's avant-garde "Heroes" music video, but the unlikely pair also made small talk about music and gathered around a piano to sing a duet, weaving together the popular song "Little Drummer Boy" with a new tune called "Peace on Earth."

In a 2014 interview quoted in the Associated Press, Crosby's daughter Mary recalled that Bowie showed up with his then-wife, Angie, dressed to the nines.

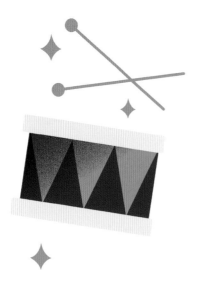

"They were both wearing full-length mink coats, they have matching full makeup, and their hair was bright red. We were thinking, 'Oh my God.'" In the end, Bowie ended up toning down his flamboyant looks, donning a casual light blue, open-collared shirt, and a trim darker blue suit jacket.

However, he wasn't so willing to compromise on the song choice, songwriter Ian Fraser told the *Washington Post* in 2006. "David came in and said, 'I hate this song. Is there something else I could sing?'" Fraser, Larry Grossman, and Alan Kohan improvised, spending 75 minutes writing "Peace on Earth" on a piano found elsewhere in the studio complex. The new composition fits seamlessly with "Little Drummer Boy"; you might even say it's one of the first prominent examples of a mash-up. But despite their different backgrounds, Bowie and Crosby sound phenomenal together. The former matches the latter's crooning note for vibrato-coated note, and his "Peace on Earth" counter-melody offers the right touch of comfort and joy.

Sadly, Crosby died of a heart attack about a month after filming *Bing Crosby's Merrie Olde Christmas.* Although the special aired in the fall, the single wasn't released until 1982, right before Bowie enjoyed a career renaissance thanks to the album *Let's Dance.* "Peace on Earth/Little Drummer Boy" proved to be quite popular in the UK, reaching No. 3 on Christmas week of that year.

In later interviews, Bowie didn't have strong memories about working on the special. However, Mary Crosby had nothing but fond memories on her end. "Dad realized David was this amazing musician, and David realized Dad was an amazing musician," she recalled. "You could see them both collectively relax and then magic was made."

HARD CANDY CHRISTMAS

1982 · DOLLY PARTON

Songwriter: Carol Hall
Also covered by: Cyndi Lauper, Kacey Musgraves, RuPaul, Tracey Thorn

CREATIVELY, things don't always go smoothly when adapting plays and musicals for the silver screen. Just ask Carol Hall. The Abilene, Texas, native wrote music and lyrics for the 1978 Broadway musical *The Best Little Whorehouse in Texas*, which was based on Larry L. King's 1974 *Playboy* article about the real-life closure of a Texas bordello. Hall's work was well-received—she won Drama Desk Awards for both Outstanding Lyrics and Outstanding Music—and the musical's actors won two Tony Awards.

In the early '80s, Dolly Parton signed on to star in the musical's film adaptation. However, changes in song selection and direction soon followed and Hall left the movie production. Luckily, the composer was upbeat about this decision in an early 1982 interview with the *Austin American-Statesman*: "Heck, they're using six of my songs. I could still win an Academy Award!" Unfortunately, none of Hall's songs received that coveted Oscar nod, although one of her compositions, "Hard Candy Christmas," has become an offbeat cult holiday favorite.

Compared favorably to Stephen Sondheim by the *New York Daily News* in 1978, the song focuses on staying upbeat even when times are tough. Like Joni Mitchell's "River," the narrator daydreams of better days (perhaps by dyeing their hair and starting over somewhere else, maybe by staying up all night staring at the stars) and ticks off a checklist for self-improvement: losing weight, sleeping more, cleaning.

The song is realistic, however; drinking too much apple wine or going bar-hopping are *also* possibilities.

Parton, whose career is full of songs about finding the silver lining despite hardships, is the perfect person to tackle "Hard Candy Christmas." Her voice bursts with pride, lending a note of optimism to the song's wry themes. Getting hard candy rather than, say, fancy chocolate for Christmas isn't something to hide; instead, it's a present to be worn as a badge of honor and survival. Fittingly, the film version of the tune boasted a genial, cinematic folk vibe that split the difference between pop and country.

"Hard Candy Christmas" appeared on the 1982 soundtrack of *The Best Little Whorehouse in Texas* and reached the top 10 of *Billboard*'s country charts. The soundtrack album fared even better, reaching No. 5 on the *Billboard* Country Album chart, although much of that success might be attributed to the LP's *other* big Parton hit: a new version of "I Will Always Love You," which became a No. 1 country single and even crossed over to the pop side.

Back in 1982, the *Austin American-Statesman* was prophetic about the musical prospects for *The Best Little Whorehouse in Texas*: "It could well be that 'Hard Candy Christmas' will achieve some kind of immortality eventually. It deserves to." As it turns out, they were right. "Hard Candy Christmas" also appeared on a reissue of the 1984 Dolly Parton and Kenny Rogers LP *Once Upon a Christmas* and would later be covered by artists such as Cyndi Lauper and Kacey Musgraves.

2000 MILES

1983 · THE PRETENDERS

Songwriter: Chrissie Hynde
Also covered by: Coldplay, Kylie Minogue, Night Flowers

THE PRETENDERS were one of the biggest rock bands of the 1980s. Led by ferocious vocalist-guitarist Chrissie Hynde, the group became known for both vulnerable pop ("Brass in Pocket") and snarling punk aggression ("Precious"). "I just do what comes naturally to me," Hynde once told *BAM*. "I don't know, it's not like, 'Oh, I've just said a few strong words, so I better get tender now.' I don't think like that. I just plug in and sing."

By late 1983, however, the Pretenders were in a transitional phase, having been dealt two tragic blows: the drug-associated deaths of guitarist James Honeyman-Scott and bassist Pete Farndon. Honeyman-Scott died in June 1982, two days after Farndon was fired from the Pretenders. The ex-bassist, meanwhile, passed in April 1983.

The Pretenders marched on, recording with new members guitarist Robbie McIntosh and bassist Malcolm Foster. Although the group scored a major hit in the US and the UK with 1982's jangly "Back on the Chain Gang," they were clearly still balancing moving on while grieving the deaths of their former bandmates. That sense of loss permeates "2000 Miles," a shimmering, languid ballad with a waltzing tempo, chiming guitars from McIntosh, and wintry percussion.

Produced by Chris Thomas, who also helmed the Pretenders hits "Talk of the Town" and "Kid," the song finds Hynde drawing on the softer and melodic side of her vocal range—an appropriate tone, as the lyrics talk about missing someone who's very far away. In fact, she sings about this person occasionally appearing to her in a dream; the insinuation is that this ephemeral appearance brings out the kind of warm feelings you experience at Christmas.

The Pretenders recorded the song at AIR Studios, which were located high above the bustling Oxford Circus in London. In the liner notes of the 2006 boxed set *Pirate Radio*, Hynde recalled being inspired by the street-level scene below her. "At the time they had these little twinkling lights, and '2000 Miles' sounds exactly how that Christmas looked." Hynde added that another influence on the song was an Otis Redding song, although nobody realized that: "Another thing I thought everyone would pick up on, and of course no one even knows that song." (In the liner notes, she called the Redding song "5000 Miles," although presumably she meant his 1968 tune "Thousand Miles Away.")

Poignantly, however, Hynde also noted that the vast distances mentioned in the song are about Honeyman-Scott. Previously, she had been more circumspect about the song's inspiration. After a performance of "2000 Miles" on the Dutch TV show *Countdown*, she looks visibly uncomfortable when asked what the song is about. At first, Hynde refuses to answer; then she says it's about "Father Christmas." Finally, when prodded again, she reluctantly says, "I wish you hadn't asked me that. Really, it's about someone who's gone, really. Let's just say it's Father Christmas."

Released as a single in the UK in November 1983, "2000 Miles" reached No. 15 on the charts. The success was a long time coming, Hynde revealed in the *Pirate Radio* liner notes: "We got the record done and gave it to the record label and they said, 'It's too close to Christmas and we can't put it out.' It was frustrating, we had to wait a year and it really bummed me out." In the US, "2000 Miles" was the B-side of the 1983 single "Middle of the Road," but has since grown into an aching holiday staple.

THANKS FOR CHRISTMAS

1983 • XTC (AKA THE THREE WISE MEN)

Songwriter: Andy Partridge

PSEUDONYMS ARE common in the music industry. Robert Zimmerman rechristened himself Bob Dylan. Vincent Furnier decided to morph into Alice Cooper. And Declan MacManus? He became Elvis Costello.

Andy Partridge, longtime leader of new wave pop geniuses XTC, is no stranger to pseudonyms. He produced music for the UK band the Woodentops using the name Animal Jesus, and dubbed himself Sandy Sandwich for an appearance on an album by experimental band the Residents. Later, Partridge assumed the nom de plume Sir John Johns in the psychedelic rock band the Dukes of Stratosphear.

However, his crowning achievement might have been coming up with the cheeky moniker Three Wise Men, which (naturally) released the single "Thanks for Christmas" in 1983. "It was written purely as a fun thing," Partridge told the XTC website Chalkhills. "I like the idea of anonymous music, and I thought I'd put together a song and then find an act to do it." XTC's then-label, Virgin Records, was in on the ruse. A news item in the *(London) Evening Standard* quoted a label employee as saying, "We've been told not to reveal who they are on pain of death. But they're all quite well-known musicians."

In reality, the members of the Three Wise Men were XTC in disguise: Partridge, Colin Moulding, and Dave Gregory. Although the band had a very distinctive sound, Partridge did his best to obscure who was behind the proverbial cloaks. He and Moulding shared the lead vocal part—a rarity, as the men usually traded off taking the spotlight. "Thanks for Christmas" also has a prominent key change, an uncommon feature of XTC songs. "But, you know, those Phil Spector kind of records have key changes," Partridge told Chalkhills. "It was done as sort of a 'what would they do' thing, and so we had a key change."

The single's B-side, "Countdown to Christmas Party Time," is a funky electro-rock song that sounds like a B-52s or Tom Tom Club outtake. And production was credited to the Three Wise Men and, jokingly, the Good Lord—aka David Lord, who co-produced Peter Gabriel's 1982 self-titled album and would later do the same on XTC's 1984 LP *The Big Express*.

"Thanks for Christmas" certainly carries on XTC's melodic pop legacy. The song comes across like a lovely snow globe, as triumphant trumpet and jolly sleigh bells combine with sparkling guitars for an atmosphere of unbridled, innocent joy. However, "Thanks for Christmas" is notable for its unique thematic content. XTC's lyrics could have a cynical edge or a clever bite, but the single is earnest to a fault; "Thanks for Christmas" overflows with gratitude for the beauty and tranquility of Christmas morning.

Word eventually leaked that Three Wise Men and XTC were one and the same; in fact, both holiday songs appeared on XTC's 1990 compilation album *Rag and Bone Buffet: Rare Cuts and Leftovers*. Partridge was also more than happy to take credit for the tune—eventually.

DO THEY KNOW IT'S CHRISTMAS?

1984 • BAND AID

Songwriters: Bob Geldof and Midge Ure
Also covered by: The *Glee* cast

CHARITY SINGLES flourished during the 1980s, as rock and pop stars of the time placed importance on giving back to people who needed a helping hand. In America, the most prominent example of this musical philanthropy was USA for Africa's 1985 benefit single "We Are the World," which featured stars like Bruce Springsteen, Cyndi Lauper, and Tina Turner joining forces to help people affected by famine in Ethiopia.

"We Are the World" followed in the footsteps of a UK charity single, "Do They Know It's Christmas?," which was recorded to raise money for the same cause. Co-written by Boomtown Rats leader Bob Geldof and Ultravox head Midge Ure, "Do They Know It's Christmas?" encourages people to be giving and generous toward those who are less fortunate. Admittedly, many of the song's lyrics haven't aged well because they rely on stereotypical descriptions of African citizens; in the modern world, we'd talk about famine and poverty using much different language. However, "Do They Know It's Christmas?" had its heart in the right place and was completely genuine about its mission.

Ure and Geldof had a compressed songwriting timeline to make a Christmas deadline, although they weren't starting completely from scratch: Geldof contributed musical ideas as well as lyrics from a tune called "It's My World" that his main band wasn't interested in recording. Ure took this foundation and ran with it, combining Geldof's ideas with his own. The song ended up including a rhythmic backdrop that included a manipulated sample of drums from Tears for Fears's "The Hurting" and live studio bass from Duran Duran's John Taylor, as well as an airy, moody synth melody.

Geldof, meanwhile, set to work recruiting star power to sing on "Do They Know It's Christmas?" Ever persuasive and passionate, he convened members of the most popular rock and pop bands of the time—not just Duran Duran but also U2, Culture Club, Spandau Ballet, and Bananarama—as well as big names such as George Michael, Sting, Jody Watley, and Paul Young. (The extended 12-inch version of the song featured a spoken-word section that included messages from even bigger megastars Paul McCartney and David Bowie.)

On November 25, 1984, this crew gathered at Sarm West Studios to record the group and solo vocals on the song. In the end, Bono, Duran Duran's Simon Le Bon, Boy George, George Michael, and Sting had memorable solo lines—and for good measure, Phil Collins also contributed live drums over the existing track. The tune ended with a huge group sing-along that reinforced the song's underlying message while also giving everyone at the session a chance to feel included.

Unsurprisingly, given the superstars involved and the good cause, "Do They Know It's Christmas?" was a commercial smash; the seven-inch alone sold 200,000 copies within its first two days on sale and easily reached No. 1 in the UK and multiple other countries around the world. In the subsequent decades, different groups of stars remade the song to benefit different causes, including a 2014 version to help those affected by the Ebola virus.

DECK THE HALLS

1984 • MANNHEIM STEAMROLLER

Songwriter: Traditional
Also covered by: Nat King Cole, Kaskade, André Rieu

CHRISTMAS MUSIC wasn't immune to advancements in technology. Just as synthesizers and digital recording techniques changed how records were made *and* how they sounded, these factors also transformed traditional holiday tunes. One of the most popular Christmas music innovators was Mannheim Steamroller. Cofounded in Omaha, Nebraska, in 1974 by composer/musicians Chip Davis and Jackson Berkey, the group became known for the long-running *Fresh Aire* series of new age albums and for groundbreaking Christmas LPs with a 20th-century spin on baroque pop.

"I wanted to explore new ways of expressing music, and created a sound I call '18th century classic rock,'" Davis once told *New Jersey Stage*. "I don't believe in all acoustic or all electronic, all digital or all analog. My style is where they all meet."

In addition to Mannheim Steamroller, Davis had another notable brush with musical fame that also shaped his style. In the 1970s, while working at an Omaha advertising agency, he created music for a character named C. W. McCall that was voiced by his coworker Bill Fries. Unexpectedly, Davis and Fries nabbed a No. 1 *Billboard* pop hit in 1976 with a song called "Convoy" that was credited to the fictional McCall. The country-

leaning tune capitalized on a fascination with truckers and trucking culture, particularly the ham radio, and also spawned a movie called *Convoy* starring Kris Kristofferson and Ali MacGraw.

This mainstream success buoyed Davis and showed him the power of possibility. In 1984, Mannheim Steamroller's *Christmas* arrived to shake up the holiday season by giving a modern polish to traditional carols. In addition to utilizing more standard instruments—guitars, strings, flute, lute, harp—the album's arrangements are dense and contain unexpected sounds. Davis is credited as playing various percussion instruments and dulcimer as well as unique items such as a pencil and dry ice. Berkey, meanwhile, plays an array of keyboards: piano, harpsichord, clavichord, toy piano, Prophet-5 synthesizer, and a Fender Rhodes.

Christmas kicked off with a galloping instrumental take on "Deck the Halls," a traditional, 16th-century Welsh carol. The combination of pulsing synths and soothing rhythmic grooves conjure the German style of music known as Krautrock, while prog-like guitars, celebratory strings, and various brassy horns pop in and out of the mix. Call it contemporary orchestral music that's more suitable for a holiday party than a solemn church service.

Improbably, *Christmas* made a big impression on both the Christmas and pop charts upon release. A glowing 1984 profile in the *Lincoln (Nebraska) Star* touted the album's pop crossover and Christmas chart success and noted that the music video for "Deck the Halls" even received airplay on various cable TV channels. Mannheim Steamroller would go on to release a string of Christmas albums after this, highlighted by 1988's *A Fresh Aire Christmas*, the group's best-selling full-length LP.

ANOTHER LONELY CHRISTMAS

1984 • PRINCE

Songwriter: Prince

FOR ALL OF PRINCE'S romantic swagger and dance-floor pizzazz, the Purple One was equally mesmerizing while mining the depths of sadness. Snowfall in April, purple rain, crying doves—life isn't always easy, and acknowledging that downside can often lead to great songs.

Originally released as the B-side to 1984's "I Would Die 4 U," Prince's "Another Lonely Christmas" lives up to its name. In fact, the song unfolds like an impossibly sad short story. First, the narrator reminisces about good times with his lady—skinny-dipping in her father's pool, playing games for money—and shares that he recently saw her sister ice skating and couldn't believe how grown-up she looked. Then "Another Lonely Christmas" takes a darker turn: It's revealed that his beloved lady died on Christmas Day seven years ago—the cause was either strep or pneumonia, though the reason is incidental—and the narrator now spends the holiday drinking too many banana daiquiris and pining for what could've been.

Prince recorded "Another Lonely Christmas" on February 18, 1984, at Sunset Sound in Hollywood, California. The sunny locale—and the fact that he tracked the upbeat, funkier tune "Pop Life" the *very next day*—didn't brighten up the music at all. "He enjoyed having his studio decorated with Christmas lights, but a traditional Christmas song wasn't something he ever pursued," wrote Duane Tudahl in the book *Prince and the Purple Rain Era Studio Sessions: 1983 and 1984*. "Instead, he decided to turn the idea of a Christmas song on its head by singing a sad song about the holiday." Performing every instrument himself, Prince crafted a tortured-soul song that feels very much like a holdover from the *Purple Rain* era. Slow-burning guitars flash like bolts of lightning, a turbulent match for his anguished vocals and instrumental flourishes like chaotic piano deconstruction. The music sounds like what grief feels like: unsettled, overwhelmed, despondent.

Despite the vivid imagery and dynamic music, Prince insisted in a 1997 online interview that "Another Lonely Christmas" is "a work of fiction." Still, the tune was so powerful he only played it live once, on December 26, 1984, at the St. Paul Civic Center Arena. "We'd like to give you a Christmas present right now," he told the crowd before the performance. "This is a new song. We've never played it before but, from us to you." The timing was poignant, of course, as the lyrics date the song as taking place the day after Christmas—while his smoldering delivery was a cathartic cleanse of the lingering sadness many feel during the season.

THANK GOD
IT'S CHRISTMAS

1984 • QUEEN

Songwriters: Brian May and Roger Taylor
Also covered by: Max Parker

CONVENTIONAL WISDOM says that New Year's Day is the perfect holiday to wipe your proverbial slate clean. That's because flipping the calendar over is symbolic: Even if you've had a run of terrible luck, a new year gives you a chance to start over and potentially have better times. Similarly, Queen's "Thank God It's Christmas" puts forth a similar argument. On Christmas Day, it's a relief to take time out to forget your worries and sadness and simply come together in celebration.

In a 2013 radio interview on *Ultimate Classic Rock Nights*, Queen guitarist Brian May revealed that drummer Roger Taylor worked up most of "Thank God It's Christmas" himself. "Except he didn't have a chorus," the guitarist noted. "So I contributed the chorus and we worked on it together, to cut a long story short." The pair then showed the music they had been working on to Freddie Mercury, who knocked his contribution out of the park. "[He] loved it and did a *beautiful* vocal," May added. "I think it's just the most understated vocal."

Mercury, who was known for his powerful operatic voice, does indeed pull back his delivery so as not to overwhelm the delicate musical undertones: lullaby-like synths, tasteful sleigh bells, honeycomb guitars. However, Mercury saves his most passionate and energetic emoting for the moments when he exclaims the song's title; he makes it clear that reaching the holiday is a relief, a milestone that deserves a special nod.

Upon release, "Thank God It's Christmas" only peaked at No. 21 in the UK, a relatively low ranking for such a big band. In the radio interview, May posited that the song's lack of a music video hurt its fortunes—a plausible explanation, especially since Queen's forward-thinking clips were always great promotional tools.

Decades later, Queen righted this wrong by releasing a video for "Thank God It's Christmas" in 2019. The gorgeous animated clip gives glimpses of residents in an apartment building, each doing their own thing on a snowy night, including a group standing on the roof admiring what looks to be the northern lights. May was pleased with the results, noting in an *NME* article that the video has "a subtle reminder that we as humans now need to feel a responsibility for the welfare of all creatures on Earth—not just for our own benefit, and that of our grandchildren, but out of respect for the rights of the animals themselves."

THE GREATEST GIFT OF ALL

1984 • KENNY ROGERS & DOLLY PARTON

Songwriter: John Jarvis

COUNTRY MUSIC is full of iconic duet partners. Tammy Wynette and George Jones. Loretta Lynn and Conway Twitty. And then there's Dolly Parton: Not only did she strike up a fruitful partnership with Porter Wagoner in the 1960s and 1970s, but she later had an even more successful collaborative relationship with Kenny Rogers. The duo first crossed paths on Parton's 1976 variety show *Dolly*, and in 1983 nabbed a major pop crossover hit with the kicky soft-pop joy "Islands in the Stream."

After the success of that song, Rogers called up Parton with another idea: doing a Christmas album together. "I was raised in a Baptist family and I've always thought of Christmas as a special time, a time when families who might be apart the rest of the year can come close together again," he told *Cash Box*. "Something special also happens when Dolly and I get together: It's a case of the whole being even greater than the sum of its parts." Parton was all-in on the concept, she added in the same *Cash Box* piece. "Kenny and I love singing together; I think the blend of our voices creates a real electricity that comes across on record. He also has a real Santa Claus spirit." The resulting collaboration ended up being released in 1984 under the title *Once Upon a Christmas*.

However, both parties first had to hammer out working details before getting started. Rogers wanted to co-produce the proposed album with songwriter/ producer David Foster, which Parton okayed as long as she could write songs for the record. "We struck this arrangement that if her songs were up to the quality of the

rest of the songs on the project then we would do them," Rogers said in the liner notes of his 1998 boxed set, *Through the Years: A Retrospective*, "and if my production was up to the rest of the production, then I could do that."

The handshake deal worked, as Rogers was thrilled with Parton's songs. He was also fond of the John Jarvis–penned soft-rock duet "The Greatest Gift of All," which sets a perfect, vivid scene: a couple who have stayed up all night after a gathering of friends and are now enjoying the calm before the Christmas morning storm. They're waiting for Santa Claus to fill stockings and add to the pile of presents under the tree. But at the moment, the world is still and quiet, save for a church bell ringing in the distance and the first signs of snow. However, the "gift" referred to in the title is the love the couple shares; that means more than any tangible present they might receive.

Through the years, "The Greatest Gift of All" was the gift that kept on giving for Parton and Rogers. "This was perhaps the most extraordinary of the songs that we recorded for the album," he said in the *Through the Years* notes, pointing out that it later became a staple of his Christmas show. "To me it deserves to be a standard." The pair performed it on their 1984 TV special, *Kenny and Dolly: A Christmas to Remember*, and it helped *Once Upon a Christmas* become a pop and country chart hit.

LAST CHRISTMAS

1984 • WHAM!

Songwriter: George Michael
Also covered by: Ariana Grande, Carly Rae Jepsen,
Jimmy Eat World, Taylor Swift

IN 1984, the pop group Wham! nabbed a string of upbeat smash hits in their native England, including the jaunty "Wake Me Up Before You Go-Go" and Motown homage "Freedom." However, the duo—school pals George Michael and Andrew Ridgeley—also had a meditative, melancholy side, as evidenced by the sensuous "Careless Whisper," which appeared on their *Make It Big* LP, and the single "Last Christmas."

Written and performed entirely by Michael, "Last Christmas" details an all-too-common holiday season experience: going to a party and running into an ex who betrayed you. The narrator understandably goes through a whirlwind of emotions upon spotting the callous deceiver—anger, bitterness, sadness, longing, resignation—before deciding that the two-timing ex is no longer worth the mental space. Instead, they close the chapter on the sour relationship and vow to be more careful with their heart in the future.

Throughout "Last Christmas," Michael writes in the first person and purposely keeps the gender of each person vague, save for one reference to a man who may be hiding part of himself. As a result, the song ends up feeling like a warm, empathetic hug to anybody who feels heartbroken and bereft during what's supposed to be a happy time.

Michael started writing "Last Christmas" on a keyboard in his childhood bedroom, after a creative lightning bolt struck in the middle of a visit with his parents. Ridgeley, who was also part of the gathering, later recalled to Smooth

Radio that his friend and bandmate slipped upstairs for about an hour and emerged with the introduction and chorus melody: "It was a moment of wonder." Michael maintained this solitude while polishing "Last Christmas" in August 1984 at London's Advision Studios, where artists such as Queen, Kate Bush, and Buzzcocks had also recorded. He worked only with engineer Chris Porter and insisted on playing every single instrument on the song by himself.

Naturally, "Last Christmas" is relatively simple, especially when compared to the maximalist pop then dominating the charts. Michael paired a holiday music staple (sleigh bells) with cutting-edge musical instruments (a LinnDrum drum machine and Roland Juno-60 synthesizer). The insistent digital rhythms add backbone to the nostalgic keyboard oscillations and Michael's honey-golden voice. "Last Christmas" twinkles with tradition but feels thoroughly modern—a fitting descriptor of Wham! and Michael's musical approach.

"Last Christmas" reached No. 2 on the UK charts upon its original release. However, in the wake of Michael's sad and unexpected 2016 death, the song has continued to connect with modern audiences. "Last Christmas" topped the UK charts in January 2021, almost 40 years after its initial release, and also hit No. 1 for two weeks in 2022. Writers have also hailed Michael's lyrics for their nuanced hints at queerness.

In 2021, Ridgeley also praised his late friend for the song's brilliance, acknowledging to Smooth Radio that the combination of seasonal cheer and unbridled longing "touched hearts" and ensured that "Last Christmas" possesses eternal resonance: "George had performed musical alchemy, distilling the essence of Christmas into music."

NO PRESENTS FOR CHRISTMAS

1985 • KING DIAMOND

Songwriters: Michael Denner and King Diamond

EVERYTHING ABOUT the Danish heavy metal band King Diamond is over the top. The group's frontman (also named King Diamond) favors elaborate face paint, an opera-shriek vocal delivery, and über-dramatic lyrics. Live, the group takes cues from Alice Cooper and plots out a prop-heavy stage configuration with hints of horror gore.

However, it's safe to say that King Diamond has been this over the top since the mid-1980s, when the band rose from the ashes of the influential heavy-metal band Mercyful Fate. King Diamond chose to issue their 1985 debut single (*debut single!*) "No Presents for Christmas" on (of all days) Christmas Day.

As the title implies, it's not a happy holiday in the King Diamond household. In a nutshell, Santa can't deliver presents because he doesn't have any help and the job is too much for one person to handle. "It is a very unique song, and there's not a lot of horror in it," King Diamond noted in an interview with the website Vanyaland. "It's kind of poking a little fun at Christmas, you know?" Indeed, the lyrics somewhat inexplicably reference the cartoon characters Donald Duck and Tom and Jerry. All are indisposed—the former's asleep, the latter are drinking—and apathy abounds.

As it turns out, King Diamond and his bandmate Michael Denner decided to write a Christmas song after Denner played him, perplexingly enough, the holiday perennial "I Saw Mommy Kissing Santa Claus." Talking to Vanyaland about the music the pair came up with, King Diamond noted, "It was supposed to be a joke, so we were just fooling around with a joke, and then it was, 'Wow, this is pretty heavy, man.'"

Musically, the song is a classic burst of explosive '80s thrash metal. At first, the song fakes out listeners by incorporating a snippet of "Jingle Bells" and "I Saw Mommy Kissing Santa Claus" at the start. However, then the song switches gears: A devilish laugh gives way to bull-charging electric guitar riffs, pounding drums, and growling vocals that rise to desperate banshee wails. In the end, "No Presents for Christmas" comes across as a cautionary tale of what happens when people ignore the spirit of Christmas and don't lend a helping hand.

WE NEED A LITTLE CHRISTMAS

1986 · JOHNNY MATHIS

Songwriter: Jerry Herman
Also covered by: Ages and Ages, Idina Menzel, the New Christy Minstrels, Kelly Rowland

BROADWAY COMPOSERS often write great Christmas songs. That's because these scribes excel at cloaking sentimentality and humor in lively music. However, the opposite fact isn't necessarily true: Broadway musicals themselves aren't always a source of great Christmas songs. A major exception to this rule, however, is 1966's *Mame* and its standout track, "We Need a Little Christmas."

Penned by Jerry Herman—a decorated composer responsible for the music and lyrics of Broadway smashes *Hello, Dolly!* and *La Cage aux Folles*—"We Need a Little Christmas" is a classic musical theater pick-me-up. The mood-lifting trimmings that

go into making the holidays great comprise the "little Christmas" referenced in the title: singing carols, lights and tinsel, slices of fruitcake, boughs of holly. The twist is that the song takes place before Thanksgiving, meaning it should be far too early to haul out the decorations and go full-on Christmas. However, the holiday represents happiness, which can be scarce in *Mame*; after all, the Great Depression looms over the musical. The message is clear: In tough times, it's perfectly acceptable to kick-start the Christmas season early—and grab your festive feelings where *and* when you can.

Appropriately, Herman ended up winning a Grammy Award for Best Score from an Original Cast Show for *Mame*. The original Broadway cast certainly helped his cause, as actors included Angela Lansbury and Bea Arthur. In fact, Lansbury sings "We Need a Little Christmas" in the original production, belting out the song with her usual indefatigable panache.

Percy Faith and the New Christy Minstrels also covered the song around the song's debut. However, another famous and enduring version comes from the Christmas crooner Johnny Mathis, who covered the song on his 1986 album *Christmas Eve with Johnny Mathis*. By that point, Mathis had three decades of holiday music success under his belt: His 1958 album *Merry Christmas* has been certified quintuple platinum and was a perennial chart hit, while his 1969 effort, *Give Me Your Love for Christmas*, was certified platinum and topped the *Billboard* Christmas Albums chart.

Christmas Eve with Johnny Mathis eventually became known for his take on "It's Beginning to Look a Lot Like Christmas," which had a prominent airing in 1992's *Home Alone 2: Lost in New York*. However, "We Need a Little Christmas" is no slouch. For starters, it has as much of a chipper attitude as Lansbury's Broadway take. Arranged by the legendary Ray Ellis, who had worked with Billie Holiday and Barbra Streisand, Mathis's version boasts a lively orchestra, full of trilling flutes and trumpets, and a huge chorus. The vocalist ties it all together with a positively jaunty vocal delivery, full of determination and confidence. No matter how impossible things might seem, Mathis is absolutely sure that giving in to the Christmas spirit will brighten the mood.

CHRISTMAS AT GROUND ZERO

1986 • "WEIRD AL" YANKOVIC

Songwriter: "Weird Al" Yankovic

DURING THE 1980s, the global threat of nuclear war seeped into the lyrics of popular music. Most of these songs understandably had a rather gloomy, fatalistic outlook; after all, there's absolutely nothing jolly about nuclear apocalypse. However, if anyone could make the world ending sound like a rousing good time, it's zany accordionist and parodist "Weird Al" Yankovic.

His "Christmas at Ground Zero" is an absurd study in contrasts. Carolers compete with warning sirens; atom bombs disrupt shopping excursions; tree trimming happens despite mushroom clouds; lovers kiss under the mistletoe even as the end is near. However, the song could also be dark: Yankovic recommends having a gun loaded and ready to use on anyone shimmying down the chimney. Somewhat incongruously, "Christmas at Ground Zero" was also inspired by old-fashioned holiday music from the 1950s and 1960s. Cheery saxophone and twinkly percussion swirl around as Yankovic sings about the world ending, adding another layer of absurdity.

Speaking to *Esquire* in 2014, Yankovic noted that "Christmas at Ground Zero" was "still very controversial" at the time. "My label didn't want me to put it out as a video because they somehow didn't feel that a song about nuclear annihilation would be very popular during the holidays. But because of my twisted sense of humor, I funded the video myself and made sure that it got out to the world." The clip plays up the push-and-pull between holiday tradition and global destruction, alternating vintage footage of happy holiday memories with atomic attacks.

Over time, the controversy around the song intensified for reasons out of Yankovic's control. In 2009, the A.V. Club pointed out that "The Night Santa Went Crazy" was on the hits compilation *The Essential "Weird Al" Yankovic*, but "Christmas at Ground Zero" didn't make the cut. Yankovic responded that he wanted to avoid "too much of an overkill on the whole Christmas thing" but also noted that "Christmas at Ground Zero" had "taken on a very *specific* connotation" due to the 9/11 terrorist attacks. "Even though the song was written in 1986, when 'ground zero' was an unspecific epicenter for nuclear annihilation . . . those were much more innocent days—I just felt that the phrase probably is not going to be part of our lexicon in that fashion for quite some time."

Unfortunately, the looming shadow of nuclear war *did* become relevant once again in 2022. Coincidentally, Yankovic spent that year touring his original music, on a trek dubbed "The Unfortunate Return of the Ridiculously Self-Indulgent Ill-Advised Vanity Tour." As a result, "Christmas at Ground Zero" was a regular part of his setlist. As he wryly put it at one tour stop, "I wrote this song in 1986. And luckily for me, it just gets more topical every year."

WINTER WONDERLAND

1987 • EURYTHMICS

Songwriters: Felix Bernard (music); Richard Bernhard Smith (lyrics)
Also covered by: Tony Bennett, Ella Fitzgerald, Darlene Love, Dean Martin

ONCE THE HOLIDAYS are over and January hits, snow is the last thing anyone wants to deal with. What looked picturesque around Christmastime now often feels like slushy drudgery—the very *opposite* of a winter wonderland.

Nevertheless, a spin or two through the song "Winter Wonderland" might return that sparkle to your eyes. The lighthearted lyrics describe how everything about life feels happier and brighter when you're in love. The lovebirds at the center of the song spend their time finding wonder in the season: taking a stroll, making a snowman, and then convening later by the fire to dream about their future plans. In this idyllic world, even the snow looks crisp and sparkling.

In 1987, the UK synth-pop act Eurythmics—the duo of Annie Lennox and Dave Stewart—recorded a very wintry-sounding version. The rhythms pitter-patter like ice pellets on a window below crystal-clear keyboards and chilly synth strings. Lennox, meanwhile, contributes a smoky, soulful vocal performance that adds just the right amount of warmth.

In a 2010 interview with the *Telegraph (UK)*, Lennox recalled that "Winter Wonderland" was "very hastily put together." She recorded it with Richard Feldman, who is also co-credited with production, drum programming, and keyboards. "We knocked it out in a day but I still think it stands up." Indeed, the song's modern sheen makes the version very distinctive. "When I listen to it, I can still hear the different flavor I wanted to give the song by putting an electro-rhythm track behind it," Lennox continued. "So you have the fusion between nostalgia and edginess, which I still think really works."

"Winter Wonderland" initially came together in 1934. Felix Bernard wrote the song's music, while Honesdale, Pennsylvania, native Richard Bernhard Smith handled the lyrics. The latter man's inspiration appeared to be twofold. According to a 2020 story in the *Tri-County Independent (Honesdale)*, written by Peter Becker—the author of *The Heritage of Dick Smith's Winter Wonderland*—Smith's sister Marjorie claimed "the beauty of the freshly fallen snow" in a park near their family home informed "Winter Wonderland." However, Richard Smith was also living with tuberculosis at the time he wrote the lyrics to "Winter Wonderland" and, sadly, he died in 1935 from the disease. Becker noted that Richard Smith's widow, Jean Connor Smith, observed that her late husband was "moved by the scene of children playing in the snow outside the windows" of a sanitarium where he was trying to convalesce from tuberculosis.

That Smith penned the fanciful song despite being so sick wasn't lost on journalist Harry Martin. In the November 29, 1934, *(Memphis) Commercial Appeal*, Martin wrote that he hoped "Winter Wonderland" would become an enduring hit "not only because it is a number with a thrill, but because its vibrant music apparently came from one whose body even as he wrote was wracked with pain."

Martin's prediction that "Winter Wonderland" deserved to become a classic turned out to be correct. "Winter Wonderland" warmed hearts in 1934—the song reached the top 5 on *Billboard*'s sheet music chart in December and opened that year's Radio City Music Hall Christmas show—and has continued to make the holidays brighter. Darlene Love's take on the song reached the top 40 of *Billboard*'s Holiday 100 chart in 2022, while Eurythmics' version also continues to be a favorite.

DO YOU HEAR WHAT I HEAR?

1987 • WHITNEY HOUSTON

Songwriters: Gloria Shayne Baker (music); Noël Regney (lyrics)
Also covered by: Glen Campbell, Kenny G, Mahalia Jackson, Patti LaBelle

WHITNEY HOUSTON possessed one of music's most singular voices. A member of a soul music family dynasty—she was the daughter of Cissy Houston and a cousin of Dionne Warwick and Dee Dee Warwick—Houston brought effortless gospel edge to her pop and R&B songs. That includes a stunning version of "Do You Hear What I Hear?" from 1987's *A Very Special Christmas*.

The song's easygoing soul-blues foundation—rat-a-tat drums, polished guitar licks, and slick keyboards—became the perfect backdrop for Houston's generous, expansive performance. "She came into the studio," *A Very Special Christmas* producer Jimmy Iovine is quoted as saying on Whitney Houston's website. "I went to get a cup of tea, and when I got back, she was finished. She sang so powerfully." Gospel-driven backing vocalists (including Darlene Love) bolster Houston's already-strong lead vocal, underscoring her dynamic prowess and rich vocal tone.

"Do You Hear What I Hear?" feels like a traditional church hymn, although the song has surprisingly modern origins. It was co-written in 1962 by the husband-wife songwriting team of Gloria Shayne Baker and Noël Regney, who also wrote "Rain Rain Go Away," a song popularized by Bobby Vinton. In their partnership, Baker generally wrote lyrics and Regney handled music, although for "Do You Hear What I Hear?" they swapped roles.

That's how Regney found himself looking for lyrical ideas after being commissioned to write a holiday song. At first, he wasn't necessarily in a festive headspace. "I had thought I'd never write a Christmas song," the *St. Anthony Messenger* magazine quoted him as saying. "Christmas had become so commercial." However, the threat of the fall 1962 Cuban Missile Crisis loomed large, he added. "In the studio, the producer was listening to the radio to see if we had been obliterated."

This terrifying time was on his mind as he walked home. Catching a glimpse of two babies with their moms, inspiration struck. "The little angels were looking at each other and smiling. All of a sudden, my mood was extraordinary," Regney recalled, and he proceeded to write song lyrics with religious allusions and imagery (e.g., lambs, shepherds) that culminate in assurances that a slumbering child will bring salvation. In other words, "Do You Hear What I Hear?" suggests that the occasion of Jesus being born could provide comfort and solace during such a fraught time. According to the couple's daughter, Gabrielle Regney, Gloria was equally inspired by the world around her: "While walking down the street in New York, my mother heard trumpets playing the melody in her head."

"Do You Hear What I Hear?" resonated with listeners. In 1962, the Harry Simeone Chorale cut a version of the tune described by *Billboard* as a "lovely and tasteful performance of a very attractive Christmas song." Two years later, Bing Crosby covered the song on *12 Songs of Christmas*, his collaborative LP with Frank Sinatra and Fred Waring and the Pennsylvanians.

Unfortunately, not every association with "Do You Hear What I Hear?" had a happy ending. Baker's 2008 obituary quoted an interview from the songwriter confirming that she and Regney later divorced. "We couldn't sing it, though. Our little song broke us up. You must realize there was a threat of nuclear war at the time."

I SAW MOMMY KISSING SANTA CLAUS

1987 · JOHN COUGAR MELLENCAMP

Songwriter: Tommie Connor
Also covered by: The Jackson 5, the Ronettes, Amy Winehouse

ON THE SURFACE, "I Saw Mommy Kissing Santa Claus" seems to be completely innocuous. Written by a London-born composer and lyricist named Tommie Connor, the song details a child who gets more than they bargained for after sneaking downstairs to look at Christmas presents: his mom kissing and tickling Santa Claus. The nosy kid swears he's going to tell his dad about what he saw—not realizing that Jolly Old Saint Nick and his father are likely one and the same.

Clever, right? Well, not everyone recognized the nuances of the song. "Ditty Rated Cheapest of Tunes Broadcast as Christmas Music" read the sub-headline of a December 19, 1952, *Cincinnati Enquirer* article, noting that "I Saw Mommy Kissing Santa Claus" was banned by a Huntington, West Virginia, radio station after listeners complained. As it turns out, people thought the song implied that Dad *isn't* dressed up as Santa Claus—meaning there's some funny business going on between Mommy and a random, red-suited man. No wonder the same *Cincinnati Enquirer* article quoted a local man saying the song was "making a mockery of decent family life as well as Christ's birthday."

Controversy aside, "I Saw Mommy Kissing Santa Claus" was an enormous commercial hit during the 1952 Christmas season, topping *Billboard*'s sheet music chart in mid-December and nabbing 12-year-old Jimmy Boyd a No. 1 single on the sales chart. Described by the *Rapid City (South Dakota) Journal* as an "amply freckled redhead who plays sturdy hillbilly music," Boyd was a Mississippi native chasing stardom in California; among other things, he appeared on Frank Sinatra's TV show. Although other people covered "I Saw Mommy Kissing Santa Claus" in 1952, Boyd's version was the most successful, selling over one million copies and becoming the biggest Christmas tune since "Rudolph, the Red-Nosed Reindeer."

Thirty-five years later, John Cougar Mellencamp decided to tackle "I Saw Mommy Kissing Santa Claus" for the charity album *A Very Special Christmas*. The Indiana rocker was having a successful 1987 thanks to the album *The Lonesome Jubilee*, which spawned the hits "Paper in Fire" and "Cherry Bomb."

Mellencamp's brisk, barnstorming take on the song was very much in line with the bar-band Americana he favored at the time. That's in large part because the recording features his then-band members: guitarists Larry Crane and Mike Wanchic; drummer Kenny Aronoff; fiddle player Lisa Germano; bassist Coby Myers; backing vocalists Crystal Taleifero and Pat Peterson; and (most prominently) jubilant accordion player John Cascella. However, in a nod to the hit Jimmy Boyd version of the song, Mellencamp also had his then–six-year-old daughter Teddi sing the last verse, in an adorably off-key voice.

These days, the song's controversial status seems to have faded away, replaced by nothing but genuine affection. "I Saw Mommy Kissing Santa Claus" has been turned into a TV movie starring Connie Sellecca and Corbin Bernsen; was the basis of a *Saturday Night Live* sketch; has been translated into several different languages; and has been covered dozens of times.

FAIRYTALE OF NEW YORK

1987 · THE POGUES FEATURING KIRSTY MACCOLL

Songwriters: Jem Finer and Shane MacGowan
Also covered by: Jon Bon Jovi, Vance Joy,
Anne-Marie and Ed Sheeran, KT Tunstall

SOME RELATIONSHIPS are distinguished by romantic situations like a coffee date or a long walk in the park. For the couple at the heart of the Pogues' "Fairytale of New York," their romance unfolds after one of them is thrown in jail to dry out after a drunken escapade. The narrator pines for his beloved, wishes them a merry Christmas, and hopes for better days.

Named after J. P. Donleavy's 1973 book of the same name, "Fairytale of New York" only becomes more bittersweet as the song progresses. The pair have a tumultuous relationship full of name-calling and mean accusations. However, there's clearly love between them, albeit love obscured by substance use and rough personalities; this affection is just a little more unorthodox than most.

"It is by far the most complicated song that I have ever been involved in writing and performing," co-writer/Pogues frontman Shane MacGowan told the *Irish Times*. "The beauty of it is that it sounds really simple."

The song's origins differ, depending on which member of the Pogues you ask. According to the *Irish Times*, the song came about either because the group rejected a manager's suggestion to cover a Christmas tune by the Band—they figured they could write a better one—or MacGowan was tackling a songwriting challenge from Elvis Costello. Costello, who produced the Pogues' 1985 LP *Rum, Sodomy and the Lash*, apparently bet MacGowan he couldn't pen a Christmas duet to sing with the bassist Cait O'Riordan.

Challenge accepted, with just a few caveats. Banjo player Jem Finer, who co-wrote the song, first had an idea that didn't stick, starring a sailor who was having a rough holiday. (His wife talked him out of that angle.) More pressingly, O'Riordan had departed the Pogues by the time the song was ready for a second voice. Luckily, the band was working with producer Steve Lillywhite, who was married to the artist Kirsty MacColl at the time. She was game to sing the proposed duet parts, providing a spunky-but-longing counter-perspective to MacGowan's gruffer, chastened voice.

With the vocals sorted, the Pogues finalized the music, which MacGowan had described to *Melody Maker* in 1985 as "like a country and Irish ballad, but one you can do a brisk waltz to," especially after you've knocked back a few. Notably, this swaying, folk-tinged song is bookended by plaintive piano at the start, and majestic strings at the end, poignant flourishes that add beauty and even wistful optimism.

"Fairytale of New York" was a roaring success upon release, reaching No. 2 in the UK. It continued to be a festive favorite: In 2011, the music licensing organization PPL determined that it was the UK's most-played Christmas song of the 21st century to date, while in 2021 the song reached No. 4 on the UK singles chart.

In spite of being so beloved, "Fairytale of New York" has stirred up controversy. In recent years, MacColl's character using a homophobic slur in the song has raised eyebrows; in fact, in 2020, BBC Radio 1 played a version that featured different lyrics. A few years before that, MacGowan clarified the usage, noting that the word choice "fitted with the way she would speak and with her character" and that the fictional woman "is not supposed to be a nice person, or even a wholesome person."

Despite the song's success, MacGowan said "Fairytale of New York" had a detrimental effect on the Pogues. "Once 'Fairytale' got big, it was really boring and you get real sick of it," MacGowan told the *Sunday Times (UK)* in the fall of 2022. "You're walking out onstage and they're applauding like mad before you've done anything, yeah? It gets frightening."

CHRISTMAS IN HOLLIS

1987 • RUN-DMC

Songwriters: Darryl "DMC" McDaniels, Jason "Jam Master Jay" Mizelle, Joseph "Rev Run" Simmons

IN 1987, the music industry producer and label executive Jimmy Iovine curated a charity album, *A Very Special Christmas*, to benefit the Special Olympics. Thanks to his clout, the compilation's tracklist featured A-list artists galore; to name a few, Madonna, Bruce Springsteen, U2, Sting, Jon Bon Jovi, and Stevie Nicks.

On Iovine's wish list also was the hip-hop trio Run-DMC. At the time, the Hollis, Queens, group was riding high on the success of the 1986 pop-rock crossover hit "Walk This Way," a collaboration with Aerosmith's Steven Tyler and Joe Perry, and influential hip-hop songs like "My Adidas." However, Darryl "DMC" McDaniels recalled that the group was lukewarm at first about contributing to *A Very Special Christmas*. "We were like, 'Nope. We're not doing it. That's what they try to do to hip-hop. They commercialize you and try to make you corny,'" he told the A.V. Club. "We're totally against anything that's going to be fake."

Run-DMC's publicist, Bill Adler, wasn't fazed by the denial. He knew he could convince the group to participate—and had an ace up his sleeve: He passed along Clarence Carter's 1968 song "Back Door Santa" to Jam Master Jay. The latter worked his magic, crafting a track that wove together the funky horns and laid-

back feel of Carter's song with shaking sleigh bells, stuttering record scratches, and interpolations of other holiday tunes: "Jingle Bells," "Joy to the World," and "Frosty the Snowman." The resulting music was anything but corny. Much as Run-DMC busted down boundaries with "Walk This Way," "Christmas in Hollis" redefined what Christmas music could sound like.

Lyrically, the song has two thematic strains. The first touts the wonderful trappings of the holidays: Mom's delicious cooking, a yule log, Christmas decorations, and gifts. The other is a whimsical story about why doing the right thing matters—and can even be lucrative. One Christmas Eve, the narrator comes upon what looks like a man and his dog in a park. As he gets closer, he realizes that the dog is a reindeer, and the man has a beard and a sack. As the clock strikes midnight, the mysterious figure disappears, leaving behind a wallet that has a million dollars and a driver's license. The name on the ID? Santa Claus. Without missing a beat, the narrator decides to mail the wallet back to Santa—it's bad luck to steal from Jolly Old Saint Nick, of course—but when he gets home, he discovers that Santa had left the money for him on purpose.

"Christmas in Hollis" never set the charts ablaze, either at the time or in the future. However, that was no measure of its impact *or* success. The tune has been used in advertisements, movies (1988's *Die Hard*), and TV shows (*The Office*), as well as sampled by other artists. Rapper Eve performed the song on *The Talk* in 2019, while Queen Latifah even teamed up with McDaniels for a performance of the song. "'Christmas in Hollis' has just become such a standard," he told the *A.V. Club*. "It's like Nat King Cole, Bing Crosby, and Run-DMC now, you know?"

MERRY CHRISTMAS BABY

1987 • BRUCE SPRINGSTEEN

Songwriters: Lou Baxter and Johnny Moore
Also covered by: Johnny Moore's Three Blazers,
Otis Redding, Ike & Tina Turner

BRUCE SPRINGSTEEN loves many things: cars, New Jersey, soul music—and Christmas tunes. The Boss is known for embracing holiday music with gusto, especially live. A muscular 1975 live take on "Santa Claus Is Comin' to Town" appeared on the B-side of the single "My Hometown." For many years, Springsteen booked December shows in Asbury Park that featured a healthy sprinkling of Christmas songs.

However, on December 28, 1980, during a run of concerts at Long Island's Nassau Veterans Memorial Coliseum, Springsteen put an E Street spin on the classic song "Merry Christmas Baby" to open the show. Burbling organ rings out first, paving

the way for Clarence Clemons's languid saxophone and setting the stage for a raspy-voiced Boss to vamp through the seductive soul tune. "All right, how'd Santa Claus treat you?" Springsteen asked the crowd at one point, drawing big cheers.

"Merry Christmas Baby" has a fascinating backstory. It first became a hit in 1947 for Johnny Moore's Three Blazers, a red-hot quartet that appeared on the cover of *Billboard* magazine that year on the strength of hits like "Moonrise" and "I'm Looking for Love." For many years, the story went that Charles Brown—the pianist-vocalist for the group—wrote "Merry Christmas Baby" at the behest of a songwriter named Lou Baxter. During a conversation with Allen Toussaint at the 1990 New Orleans Jazzfest, Brown talked about how this conversation with Baxter went down.

"He said, 'Charles, if you could do one of my numbers, I could get a $500 advance. I need it because I need a throat operation.' I said, 'Lou, let me look into your satchel and see what you have.'" Brown said he discovered a song called "Merry Christmas Blues," and while he wasn't totally enamored of the song, it did inspire him to mold it into a different song, called "Merry Christmas Baby." Upon release, however, the song was credited to Lou Baxter—and, curiously enough, Blazers member Johnny Moore. Brown's name was nowhere to be found.

Years later, a writer for the *Smithsonian* did some digging and discovered some other complicating facts. Baxter was actually a nom de plume used by an Army veteran named Andrew Whitson Griffith, who was an aspiring songwriter on the Los Angeles blues scene. Griffith copyrighted a song called "Merry Xmas Baby" in September 1947, but it remained unpublished. However, lyrics to this version stored at the Library of Congress showed marked similarities to the final "Merry Christmas Baby" recorded by Johnny Moore's Three Blazers. In other words, Brown likely edited this version of the song—and deserved some recognition for his role in the tune.

No matter what the provenance, "Merry Christmas Baby" and its lovestruck lyrics are timeless and strike a nerve. As for Bruce Springsteen and the E Street Band, they played the song twice more that week in 1980, including on New Year's Eve, but then wouldn't perform it live again until 1994. However, the live version of "Merry Christmas Baby" on *A Very Special Christmas* cemented the Boss's Christmas season pedigree for good.

PUT A LITTLE LOVE IN YOUR HEART

1988 • AL GREEN & ANNIE LENNOX

Songwriters: Jackie DeShannon, Jimmy Holiday, Randy Myers
Also covered by: Mahalia Jackson

COUNTLESS MOVIES and TV shows have adapted the premise of Charles Dickens's *A Christmas Carol*: Someone who is selfish and ill-tempered changes their ways after being visited by the ghosts of their past, present, and future lives. For example, it's the plot device driving the 1988 movie *Scrooged,* which stars Bill Murray as a TV bigwig who eventually gets his holiday mojo back after being shown some very sobering potential future scenes.

The *Scrooged* soundtrack was quite eclectic, featuring songs by rapper Kool Moe Dee, the Band's Robbie Robertson, and R&B star Natalie Cole. The compilation's lead-off tune especially turned some heads: Eurythmics vocalist Annie Lennox and soul legend Al Green doing a midtempo cover of Jackie DeShannon's "Put a Little Love in Your Heart."

"People said you can't sing with Annie Lennox. That's wrong for you to do that," Green told the *Birmingham (Alabama) Post-Herald*, as quoted in Jimmy McDonough's book, *Soul Survivor: A Biography of Al Green.* The offended parties, he said? "Some people in the church." Despite these misgivings, Lennox and Green sounded note-perfect together, bringing positive vibes to the gospel-influenced version. And while the song isn't explicitly about Christmas, its message—choose kindness and love, as that makes everything better—certainly dovetails with seasonal blessings.

DeShannon initially co-wrote "Put a Little Love in Your Heart" with her brother, Randy Myers, and the songwriter Jimmy Holiday. "I was just writing for this album that was up and coming, and that was one of the songs," DeShannon told SongFacts. "My brother Randy was playing this little riff and I said, 'Gee, I really like that riff, that's great.'"

DeShannon, who was previously known for her 1965 hit "What the World Needs Now Is Love," immediately came up with the song's first two lines. "I owe some of that to my mom, because she was always saying that people should put a little love in their heart when things are not so good," she continued. "I'd like to say it was very difficult, but it was one of those songs you wait a lifetime to write." Sunny and upbeat, DeShannon's "Put a Little Love in Your Heart" became a huge hit, reaching No. 4 on the *Billboard* Hot 100 in 1969.

Nearly two decades later, Lennox and Green also enjoyed great success with "Put a Little Love in Your Heart," as their version reached No. 9 on the same chart, Green's first top 10 hit since 1974. Decades later, in her SongFacts interview, DeShannon was delighted with the success of this cover and how the song itself earned a place in pop culture, such as on *American Idol* and through usage in ads. "It's definitely the gift that keeps on giving."

DRIVING HOME FOR CHRISTMAS

1988 · CHRIS REA

Songwriter: Chris Rea
Also covered by: Engelbert Humperdinck

IT'S SAFE TO SAY that Chris Rea wasn't having the best Christmas season in 1978. His manager dumped him. His record deal was on shaky ground; in fact, he was even considering getting out of the business and opening an Italian restaurant. Getting home for the holidays was also a challenge because he couldn't drive—and, to add insult to injury, his label wouldn't pony up for a train ticket.

Nevertheless, Rea was undaunted by his woes—and determined to come home. His wife drove to London's Abbey Road Studios from their place in Middlesbrough in North Yorkshire, England—a trip that took well over four hours—to fetch Rea. The couple then headed straight back home, naturally as it began snowing and making the roads absolutely treacherous.

"We kept getting stuck in traffic and I'd look across at the other drivers, who all looked so miserable," Rea told the *Guardian* in 2016. "Jokingly, I started singing: 'We're driving home for Christmas . . .' Then, whenever the streetlights shone inside the car, I started writing down lyrics."

After arriving home, his fortunes turned around. He received a check for £15,000 (more than £110,000 in 2023) because his song "Fool (If You Think It's Over)" had become a top 20 US pop hit. In early 1979, that was also followed by a Grammy nomination for Best New Artist. Rea stashed away the song lyrics he had scribbled down on the ride home for another day.

However, Rea never forgot about the song idea. Years later, he and a keyboardist named Max Middleton were breaking in two new Roland digital pianos. As Rea recalled in a 2019 interview on his YouTube channel, the men agreed that they could measure the quality of the pianos by playing Count Basie–like pieces on the instruments. The resulting improvised music reminded him of his long-ago Christmas lyrics. He dusted them off and discovered that the sentiments fit the music perfectly.

And so "Driving Home for Christmas" ended up a laid-back, jazzy song that feels like a solo driver narrating his harried jaunt home. Rea sings of hitting red lights and traffic jams, and longing for the freeway, which is his quick ticket to get there faster. As he sings, he sees that the other drivers around him are just as frazzled and focused on the drive—a powerful statement about how we're not as alone in the world as we think we are.

"Driving Home for Christmas" initially surfaced as the B-side of Rea's 1986 single "Hello Friend." The festive song caught the ear of a radio DJ, who played it instead of the single's A-side. "Don't ask me why—I have no idea," Rea shared in the YouTube interview. "There wasn't a penny's worth of promotion [that] went into it. In fact, it wasn't the type of thing we were doing at that time." Rea added that he and Middleton even considered sending "Driving Home for Christmas" to Van Morrison, with the idea the Irish singer would cover the song: "That's why it's in that key—'cause it's Van Morrison's key."

Still, Rea re-cut the song himself and "Driving Home for Christmas" was reissued as a proper single in 1988. The song only reached No. 53 in the UK during its initial run, but has grown in popularity over the years to become a perennial hit: It reached the UK top 40 during the 2007 holiday season and peaked at No. 10 in late 2021.

Incredibly enough, Rea resisted making the song a live staple for many years. When he did finally dust off the song again, he went all-out. During a December 2014 show at London's Eventim Apollo, he rented a dozen snow cannons that propelled three feet of fake snow over the delighted crowd. The cleanup tab, Rea revealed to the *Guardian*? A whopping £12,000—a figure more than $17,000 in 2023.

MERRY CHRISTMAS (I DON'T WANT TO FIGHT TONIGHT)

1989 · RAMONES

Songwriter: Joey Ramone
Also covered by: Little Steven and the Disciples of Soul, Mattiel, PINS

WE SHOULD HAVE expected that a holiday with the legendary punk band the Ramones wouldn't come off without a hitch. However, "Merry Christmas (I Don't Want to Fight Tonight)" makes a valiant attempt at keeping the peace around the holidays. In fact, the Ramones explicitly say the holiday's not the time for a breakup. Instead, the narrator serves up reminders of Christmas bliss: He's looking for Santa; mentions the innocent children fast asleep, excited about the holiday; and expresses love for his partner.

"Merry Christmas (I Don't Want to Fight Tonight)" first emerged as the B-side of "I Wanna Live," a single from the band's 1987 album *Halfway to Sanity*. Two years later, the band elevated the song to album status, including it on 1989's *Brain Drain*. Jean Beauvoir, who played bass for the outrageous New York City hard

rock band the Plasmatics, produced and contributed guitar to "Merry Christmas (I Don't Want to Fight Tonight)." Still, the midtempo song isn't as aggressive as other Ramones tunes. In a nod to the holiday theme, the tune combines hot-rodding guitar riffs with prominent sleigh bells and a vocal take by Joey Ramone that's rough-hewn but full of heart.

The "Merry Christmas (I Don't Want to Fight Tonight)" video received airplay on MTV's alternative music specialty video show *120 Minutes*. Directed by George Seminara and filmed at New York's Cine-Studio, the video alternates between live shots of the Ramones playing with footage of a couple fighting during their Christmas party, as their guests look on in befuddlement. Notably, bassist C. J. Ramone appeared in the song's video, as original member Dee Dee Ramone had left the band not long before.

As it turns out, the combined success of "Merry Christmas (I Don't Want to Fight Tonight)" and the band's Stephen King movie theme song "Pet Sematary" ended up helping *Brain Drain* become what was then the Ramones' best-selling album to date. The song also later appeared on the Steven Van Zandt–curated soundtrack to 2004's *Christmas with the Kranks*.

MISTRESS
FOR CHRISTMAS

1990 • AC/DC

Songwriters: Angus Young and Malcolm Young
Also covered by: Halestorm

AC/DC ARE KNOWN as a serious band with a catalog full of no-nonsense songs about riding highways to hell and dodging explosive substances. Live, the Australian group also is quite serious about rocking—after all, they often have a gigantic bell lowered from the stage for the hit "Hells Bells," to make the song that much more epic.

In 1990, AC/DC released *The Razors Edge*, a blockbuster featuring what would become one of their biggest singles, the pulverizing "Thunderstruck." More curiously, however, the album also featured a song called "Mistress for Christmas." Musically, it's a classic AC/DC bluesy rocker with laid-back grooves, plenty of gargantuan riffs, and Angus Young's inimitable yowl. However, the lyrics are quite cheeky, with references to romps in bed (including a threesome) and double entendres equating various Christmas images with sexual acts. In a 1991 interview with *Guitar World*, guitarist Angus Young called "Mistress for Christmas" the "funniest song" on *The Razors Edge*.

He then revealed that the lyrics had a rather unexpected inspiration: the future 45th president of the US, Donald Trump. "He was big news at the time, so we thought we'd have a bit of fun and humor with it," Young noted. It wasn't for Trump's politics, however. Back then, the gossip mags were abuzz that he was having an affair with a woman named Marla Maples.

With that context in mind, "Mistress for Christmas" makes a lot more sense, as there are also veiled references to being rich and lyrics that seem to poke fun at the callous ways some men treat women; after all, the idea that someone would ask for (or receive!) a mistress as a gift is gauche. In short, although "Mistress for Christmas" might seem like a lighthearted throwaway, under the surface AC/DC put together a rather pointed critique of fame and fortune. Now *that's* rock 'n' roll.

CHRISTMAS ALL OVER AGAIN

1992 • TOM PETTY & THE HEARTBREAKERS

Songwriter: Tom Petty
Also covered by: Jon Bon Jovi, Goo Goo Dolls, Darlene Love

WHEN JIMMY IOVINE started compiling a sequel to his *A Very Special Christmas* album in the early 1990s, his target contributor list included Tom Petty. The two men were longtime friends who had crossed paths professionally for decades; as an example, Iovine co-produced Tom Petty & the Heartbreakers' 1979 breakthrough *Damn the Torpedoes*. "When he said to me, 'I'll write my own song,' I said, 'Okay,'" Iovine later recalled. "If anybody can write a Christmas song, he can."

Petty came through mightily with a droll song called "Christmas All Over Again." It's a somewhat meta song, proclaiming that the holiday is here, with all that entails: relatives you're (mostly) happy to see, kids having a blast, smooching under the mistletoe, racing to get shopping done. Overall, however, "Christmas All

Over Again" is thrilled that the holiday comes once a year—after all, the tune ends with Petty ticking off his Christmas wish list, which includes (of course) a guitar, as well as other musical instruments and Chuck Berry sheet music.

Petty wrote "Christmas All Over Again" on a ukulele given to him by George Harrison. The former Beatle "spent a whole afternoon teaching me the chords," Petty recalled in the liner notes of Tom Petty & the Heartbreakers' 1995 *Playback* boxed set. "The ukulele is a really cool instrument, even though it doesn't have that image."

As with so many other holiday tunes, "Christmas All Over Again" came together during the summer, after Petty and his uke headed to Florida. The rocker remained determined to come up with an original song, he said in *Playback*, and had a specific vision in mind. "To me and Mike [Campbell] there's only one Christmas album in the pop field, and that's Phil Spector's [*A Christmas Gift for You from Phil Spector*]. That was the only one we could relate to. That really sounds like Christmas to me."

Petty decided to emulate the lush, expansive sound on *A Christmas Gift for You from Phil Spector*, which meant hiring an ensemble of musicians and recording the song. Luckily, Jimmy Iovine loved the idea and helped find the musicians—which, as Petty recalls, included a harpist and a harpsichordist, two bassists, four acoustic guitarists, and guest session drummer Jim Keltner complementing Stan Lynch.

With such a huge cast of players, "Christmas All Over Again" does indeed have an old-fashioned, classic Christmas musical feel. Guitars chime and ring like church bells; drums pound and clop like horse hooves; and a harp adds twinkle in the background. Petty matches the mood by affecting his most reverent croon, as if he's presiding over the holiday festivities, rather than just participating in them. The song ended up appearing in 1992's *Home Alone 2: Lost in New York*, while Tom Petty & the Heartbreakers performed the song live in 2000 at the White House, for the *A Very Special Christmas from Washington, D.C.* TV special.

SLEIGH RIDE

1992 • TLC

Songwriters: Leroy Anderson (music);
Lisa "Left Eye" Lopes; Mitchell Parish (lyrics)

DURING THE 1990s, musicians weren't afraid to tamper with tradition. Nirvana upended rock 'n' roll, of course, but countless other artists also took a crack at updating classics. Case in point: Early in their career, the hip-hop trio TLC completely overhauled the mid-20th-century hit "Sleigh Ride" for modern audiences.

Originally, the tune was a straightforward (if whimsical) song about a laid-back winter sleigh excursion, with galloping music by Leroy Anderson and jaunty lyrics by Mitchell Parish. TLC draws on this source material somewhat—their version boasts the requisite festive percussion, and Tionne "T-Boz" Watkins references the original "Sleigh Ride" lyrics in the first chorus of the song—although their take is very much in line with the groove-heavy R&B and hip-hop popular in the early '90s. In fact, "Sleigh Ride" wouldn't sound out of place on TLC's smash debut album, 1992's *Ooooooohhh . . . On the TLC Tip.*

It helped that the song was produced by Organized Noize, an Atlanta-based team who worked with OutKast and Xscape in addition to TLC. Co-production came from TLC's then-manager, Pebbles, who had experienced her own success during the 1980s with "Mercedes Boy." Together, they created a musical showcase that gave each member of TLC a chance to shine. Lisa "Left Eye" Lopes turns in several cheeky rap interludes that show off her gift for wordplay (including references to a flirtatious Santa), while Rozonda "Chilli" Thomas sings the tune's hook, which offers Christmas and New Year's greetings. T-Boz, meanwhile, keeps the positive vibe going, rapping hints that the holiday is for cozying up with a beloved crush.

TLC's "Sleigh Ride" initially appeared on 1992's *Home Alone 2: Lost in New York* soundtrack—fittingly, the song's lyrics make a reference to the film—but also became an integral track on 1993's *A LaFace Family Christmas*, a holiday album released by the band's label, LaFace Records. On that record, TLC appeared next to future stars Usher, OutKast, and Toni Braxton, performing not just "Sleigh Ride" but also "All I Want for Christmas."

ALL I WANT FOR CHRISTMAS IS YOU

1994 • MARIAH CAREY

Songwriters: Walter Afanasieff and Mariah Carey
Also covered by: August Burns Red, Fifth Harmony, CeeLo Green, My Chemical Romance

MARIAH CAREY wasn't overselling herself or responding to frivolous litigation when she attempted (and failed) to trademark the phrase "Queen of Christmas" in 2022.

The pop icon has become an emblem of everything that's great and uplifting about the holidays because of her mammoth 1994 song "All I Want for Christmas Is You."

At the time the song was released, Carey was already a major pop star, having released three hit full-length albums since 1990. Recording a Christmas album wasn't even on her radar yet. "Originally, I was like, 'This is a little bit too early in my career to do a Christmas album,'" she confessed to *USA Today* in 2019. "I didn't understand why it was being suggested to me." She loved the holiday, of course—but a challenging upbringing meant that her version of Christmas might be far different from the one experienced by many other people. "I grew up not having a lot of money and not being able to experience it like the other kids did," she continued. "I wanted Christmas to be perfect, but for a lot of different reasons, it didn't always end up working out well."

That formative experience infused the song's lyrics and music. Co-written with her then–frequent songwriter collaborator Walter Afanasieff—among their co-compositions are Carey's smashes "Hero" and "One Sweet Day"—"All I Want for Christmas Is You" is a love song masquerading as a holiday tune. Carey reiterates time and time again that her wish list is modest: The only thing on it is her beloved, and she'll be patiently hanging out underneath the mistletoe waiting for them until they arrive. In fact, being with her person means more to her than receiving presents and Santa bringing toys; Carey even promises she won't stay up late and listen for reindeer. The overarching message is that tangible things aren't as meaningful around the holidays as being with the people you love.

"All I Want for Christmas Is You" pairs its sweet sentiments with equally sugar-frosted music. The song begins with what sounds like the pirouetting melody from a windup music box. From there, Carey does one of her famous dramatic, big-voiced crescendos before the song takes off, thanks to relentlessly upbeat piano, soul-buoyed backing vocalists, and an explosion of sleigh bells. It's simultaneously both vintage-sounding and modern, which no doubt explains its popularity.

The lone bit of dissension with "All I Want for Christmas Is You" is how it initially came about. Carey has said she started writing the song herself on a Casio keyboard, with the film *It's a Wonderful Life* on as background ambience. However, Afanasieff told the *New York Times* the origins were more collaborative. "I sat at the piano with Mariah in the room, and I started plunking out—like I always did, on every single song we've ever written together—a particular chord." That led to the familiar music we all know and love today.

"All I Want for Christmas Is You" is inarguably considered one of the greatest (if not *the* greatest) modern original holiday songs. Incredibly enough, back in 1994 it wasn't released as a commercial single, but instead was sent to top 40 and adult contemporary radio stations. Carey also downplayed the original songs on her Christmas album, telling *Billboard* at the time, "It was definitely a priority for me to write at least a few new songs, but, for the most part, people really want to hear the standards at Christmas, no matter how good a new song is."

As we know now, "All I Want for Christmas Is You" became the rare new song that evolved into a standard. It took some nudging from pop culture—notably an appearance in 2003's cult holiday film *Love, Actually*—and 25 years, but the tune finally reached No. 1 on the *Billboard* Hot 100 in late December 2019. The song has reached this peak again in each subsequent year and was the first holiday single certified diamond, for 10 million copies sold.

But "All I Want for Christmas Is You" isn't just wildly popular. It's a bona fide holiday phenomenon and tradition that's spawned memes, books, tours, a film, sing-alongs, and more. Carey's embraced them all: On Halloween night 2022, she posted a black-and-white video of herself exercise-biking while wearing a witch's hat and a latex catsuit. As she cackled mightily, calendar pages flew around her head like bats. After the November 1 page flapped by, the video flipped into a full-color clip of Carey: Wearing her fur-trimmed Christmas gear, she sings, "It's tiiiiime!" in a high-pitched trill as a lead-in to a snippet of "All I Want for Christmas Is You."

In other words, it's not a stretch to say Carey's entire identity has become synonymous with the Christmas season—and she wouldn't have it any other way. "When I see people dancing in the streets to the song and having these big, huge festivals, and they're playing it, it's what [the] holidays mean to me," she told Apple

Music's Zane Lowe in 2020. "I have so many memories attached to the song, but people come to me and tell me about their memories. And that's what means the most."

OI TO THE WORLD!

1996 • THE VANDALS

Songwriter: Joe Escalante
Also covered by: No Doubt

ON THE SURFACE, punk and Christmas songs seem like oil and water: They just don't mix. However, Orange County, California, punk band the Vandals beg to differ. In 1996, they thumbed their nose at tradition and released a Christmas album, *Oi to the World! (Christmas with the Vandals)*.

"We talked about it for years and we'd sit bored in the van driving around for hours and hours and making up silly Christmas songs," guitarist Warren Fitzgerald said in 1999. "We thought, 'Hey, there hasn't been a punk Christmas record for a long time.'" Recorded in April 1996 for roughly $2,000, the album features dark-humored punk songs with a Christmas twist.

The de facto title track of the album was the hard-charging, wiry "Oi to the World!" It wasn't a punk-i-fied cover of "Joy to the World," however, but a song referencing a style of punk music known as Oi! that started in the UK in the late '70s that was meant to be inclusive of different groups of people.

The Vandals song features a punk named Haji who wears a turban and plays in an Oi! band. One Christmas Eve, he runs into a skinhead named Trevor down at the pub. Trevor isn't exactly the accepting type; in fact, he assaults Haji by yanking off his turban. That kicks off a chain of events that leads to the two men having a rooftop fight on Christmas. Trevor does damage with nunchucks, but Haji almost mortally wounds his enemy with a sword. In the end, however, he saves Trevor by using his turban as a tourniquet—and the two punks mend fences over some bourbon at the pub. The chorus is far more lighthearted, musing that if God saw what was going on, he'd shout out both sides (the punks and the skins) and encourage people to embrace the unifying force of Oi! music.

No Doubt—who were buds with the Vandals—covered "Oi to the World!" in 1997. Unfortunately, this rendition didn't necessarily boost the reputation (or commercial impact) of the Vandals' LP. "That record sold worse than any record we've ever done," Fitzgerald told *Lollipop* magazine in 2000. "By a long shot." In response, the Vandals reissued the LP under a slightly new name (*Oi to the World!*) with a new cover and a bonus track. "That's why we recently repackaged it so it wouldn't look like a Christmas record, even though it is," Fitzgerald quipped. "Now we hopefully won't get all the returns on December 27th."

CHRISTMAS EVE/ SARAJEVO 12/24

1996 • TRANS-SIBERIAN ORCHESTRA

Songwriters: Robert Kinkel, Jon Oliva, Paul O'Neill

CAN HARD ROCK and the holidays coexist in harmony? With a fierce headbang and squealing guitar solo, the Trans-Siberian Orchestra answers with a resounding yes.

Since forming in 1996 as a side project of the cult metal band Savatage, the troupe has become a Christmas force that tours North American arenas each year with an impressive stage production and a repertoire full of covers and originals.

The Trans-Siberian Orchestra's signature song is a combination of both: a thundering, guitar-heavy instrumental called "Christmas Eve/Sarajevo 12/24" that combines elements of "God Rest Ye Merry Gentlemen" and the Ukrainian song "*Shchedryk,*" which eventually became better known as "Carol of the Bells" (see page 196). It's inarguably one of the most intense Christmas songs ever written, as it contains pounding drums, a twin electric guitar blast, and dynamic orchestral roars. However, "Christmas Eve/Sarajevo 12/24" also makes room for more delicate moments, like a fluttering flute, and its emotional heart is a cello playing "God Rest Ye Merry Gentlemen" in a mournful, lonely tone.

In a 2003 *Christianity Today* interview, Savatage producer and Trans-Siberian Orchestra founder Paul O'Neill said that the song was based on a true story, a cellist who played Christmas carols in Sarajevo during the Bosnian War in the midst of bombed-out devastation. "The orchestra represents one side, the rock band the other, and the single cello represents that single individual, that spark of hope," he explained. O'Neill's details were slightly off, but the song's premise is loosely based on the true story of Vedran Smailović, a cellist from Bosnia and Herzegovina who played Albinoni's "Adagio in G minor" for 22 days straight during the Bosnian War's siege of Sarajevo.

The song first appeared on Savatage's 1995 album *Dead Winter Dead* under the name "Christmas Eve (Sarajevo 12/24)." It was popular during that holiday season and even reached the top 40 of *Billboard*'s Hot Adult Contemporary chart. However, the tune's popularity exploded after reappearing on Trans-Siberian Orchestra's 1996 debut, *Christmas Eve and Other Stories.* It ended up charting on the overall *Billboard* Hot 100 twice, barely missing the top 40 each time. In 2016, "Christmas Eve/Sarajevo 12/24" was also named the third-best-selling digital single of all time, with sales of 1.3 million copies.

I WON'T BE HOME FOR CHRISTMAS

1997 • BLINK-182

Songwriters: Tom DeLonge, Mark Hoppus, Scott Raynor

AT CHRISTMAS, people tend to sweep bad feelings and grudges under the rug for the sake of keeping the peace. Not the members of Blink-182: Across the board, their holiday songs pull no punches, brutally telling off their haters. "Happy Holidays, You Bastard" is a very not-safe-for-work tune about giving a present to someone you despise, and saying they'll only mend fences if some graphic sexual acts occur.

Co-written by vocalist/guitarist Tom DeLonge and vocalist/bassist Mark Hoppus and former drummer Scott Raynor, "I Won't Be Home for Christmas" seems to start out peacefully, with a lighthearted rendition of "Deck the Halls." The tune then jumps right into Blink-182's trademark pop-punk jawing—and some rather curmudgeonly lyrics about wanting to be left alone during the holiday. More specifically, the narrator is super-annoyed by a group of Christmas carolers and decides to go after them with a baseball bat. Unsurprisingly, this doesn't go over well; in fact, the bat-wielding crank gets tossed in jail and will miss the holiday unless someone posts bail. (And, in true Blink-182 fashion, the song's ultimate twist is the Christmas gift he receives is jailhouse affection.)

Hoppus sings "I Won't Be Home for Christmas" in a deadpan voice, which only amplifies the narrator's lack of remorse. However, the song ends with Hoppus and DeLonge singing the titular lyric together, in a shower of pulverizing drums and sleigh bells—creating a weird sense of pride about the situation.

The song was hugely popular in Canada and became Blink-182's only No. 1 single there, staying atop the charts for five weeks in 2001 and 2002. Despite such success, time hasn't softened the band's stance toward Christmas: In 2019, Blink-182 returned with "Not Another Christmas Song," which celebrates another year not being six feet under (really) and suggests that perhaps the best gift for one unhappy couple is a divorce.

I WANT AN ALIEN FOR CHRISTMAS

1997 • FOUNTAINS OF WAYNE

Songwriters: Chris Collingwood and Adam Schlesinger

KIDS LOVE putting curveballs on their Christmas lists—dream gifts that are a long shot or presents that are way out of reach, whether due to price range or something else. It's safe to say that "I Want an Alien for Christmas," by the power-pop band Fountains of Wayne, falls into the "something else" category.

Co-produced and co-written by band members Adam Schlesinger and Chris Collingwood, the song tells Santa not to bring the usual suspects—bicycles, basketballs, sweaters—and instead deliver a cute green flying alien with 17 eyes. The narrator swears they'll take good care of the alien (he even has a bathtub where the alien can stay!) and that the creature will never be left alone. Musically, "I Want an Alien for Christmas" is pure Fountains of Wayne–caliber pop, with droll vocals, chugging guitars, retro keyboards, and an explosive chorus with earnest

harmonies. Call it a hip '90s update of "I Want a Hippopotamus for Christmas"—and a catchy Christmas earworm full of goofy verve.

Incredibly enough, Fountains of Wayne almost didn't record the song. "Our friend Steve Greenberg was working with Hanson, who were making a Christmas album," Schlesinger wrote in the liner notes to Fountains of Wayne's 2005 rarities album, *Out-of-State Plates*. "I gave a demo of this song to him to pass along." Hanson turned the song down, so Fountains of Wayne instead cut the song themselves on a day off at Liverpool, England's Elevator Studios, during the summer of 1997. Backed by another holiday song, "Man in the Santa Suit," it became one of the group's most popular songs in the UK, reaching No. 36 in late 1997.

MERRY CHRISTMAS, HAPPY HOLIDAYS

1998 • NSYNC

Songwriters: JC Chasez, Vincent Degiorgio, Veit Renn, Justin Timberlake
Also covered by: David Archuleta, Betty Who, Pentatonix

LET'S FACE IT, anticipating Christmas is almost as exciting as the actual holiday itself. That's the underlying message of NSYNC's "Merry Christmas, Happy Holidays," which appeared on the group's 1998 album *Home for Christmas.*

A classic R&B soul song in the vein of Donny Hathaway or Stevie Wonder, the tune first describes two things that make the holidays great: being out of school and a perfect snowy Christmas Eve night, where the stockings are neatly hung up and ready for Santa. Not only will the forthcoming pile of presents make kids happy, but this scene also represents the love and togetherness permeating Christmas. In fact, while "Merry Christmas, Happy Holidays" later makes a direct reference to God, the tune stresses that it doesn't matter *how* or *what* you celebrate—the Christmas spirit and being with family you love is what will bring you joy. NSYNC's gorgeous multi-part harmonies give way to a gospel choir as the song ends, reinforcing the song's spiritual, exuberant vibe.

NSYNC members JC Chasez and Justin Timberlake co-wrote "Merry Christmas, Happy Holidays" with Veit Renn and Vincent Degiorgio. Degiorgio is credited with signing the group to RCA Records for North America, after being blown away by a Budapest, Hungary, NSYNC concert. On the same night Degiorgio told a colleague they had to release the group's album, he also made another bold proclamation, as noted in a 2013 interview: "I said, 'If they let me put this record out, I'm not only going to have a hit with it, we're also going to do a Christmas record.'"

Mission accomplished. As it turned out, "Merry Christmas, Happy Holidays" was well-timed: It arrived at the end of NSYNC's breakthrough year in America. In addition to appearing on *Home for Christmas*, the song was included in a 1998 Disney Christmas movie *I'll Be Home for Christmas* and appeared on *Billboard*'s Top 40 Mainstream chart. Fittingly, in December of that year, the video for "Merry Christmas, Happy Holidays" also reached No. 1 on MTV's then-new daily countdown show *Total Request Live*.

8 DAYS OF CHRISTMAS

2001 • DESTINY'S CHILD

Songwriters: Beyoncé Knowles, Errol McCalla Jr., Kelly Rowland

MUCH LIKE TLC'S "Sleigh Ride," Destiny's Child's "8 Days of Christmas" is a blend of the classic and contemporary. The trio—Beyoncé Knowles, Kelly Rowland, and Michelle Williams—put a unique spin on a Christmas standard, drawing on traditional source material ("12 Days of Christmas") to create an entirely different, modern holiday tune.

"8 Days of Christmas" originally surfaced on a deluxe edition of 1999's *The Writing's on the Wall* before reemerging as the title track of the group's 2001 holiday album; that album featured new takes on "White Christmas" and "Little Drummer Boy" as well as originals. "There hasn't been a Christmas album like this—it's kind of like a 2000 version of *Motown Christmas*," Knowles told MTV in 2001. "There's nothing traditional about the album, even with the traditional songs. We totally remade them, and we have some really different harmonies and arrangements."

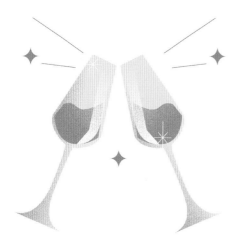

"8 Days of Christmas" overflows with gratitude for the generous spirit of a boyfriend, who doles out daily thoughtful gifts. These presents may be expensive and grand—for example, a Mercedes and designer sunglasses—but are generally more personal: a handwritten poem, a foot massage, a gift certificate earmarked for CDs, a romantic dinner. The music was very much of a piece with Destiny's Child's hit singles of the time, with dramatic synth strings and red-hot beats laying a foundation for the trio's lilting, pinpoint harmonies.

Destiny's Child performed the song live multiple times, helping *8 Days of Christmas* reach the top 40 on *Billboard*'s album chart, but still embarked on a planned break to do solo projects afterward. Fans never forgot Destiny's Child's holiday gift, however—*8 Days of Christmas* was finally certified platinum in 2020.

GOD REST YE MERRY GENTLEMEN

2002 • BARENAKED LADIES & SARAH McLACHLAN

Songwriter: Traditional
Also covered by: Garth Brooks, Nat King Cole,
Pentatonix, Trans-Siberian Orchestra

THE EARLY 2000s ushered in another holiday music boom, as the then-burgeoning underground pop and rock scenes fully embraced the spirit of the holidays. The popularity of the punk-leaning Vans Warped Tour prompted the release of 2003's *A Santa Cause: It's a Punk Pop Christmas*, while indie rockers gathered for 2001's *Stuck in the Chimney (More Christmas Singles)*. And then there was the popular teen drama *The O.C.*, which released 2004's *Have a Very Merry Chrismukkah*, featuring Low, Jimmy Eat World, and others.

Perhaps the most formative (and comprehensive) 2000s alternative Christmas music collections emerged courtesy of the label Nettwerk Records, which issued a series of albums under variations on the name *Maybe This Christmas*. These compilations featured a who's who of current *and* future stars: Coldplay, Avril Lavigne, Rilo Kiley, Ben Folds, and Phantom Planet.

But the most inspired (and enduring) part of the *Maybe This Christmas* universe was a unique mash-up cover of the traditional English carol "God Rest Ye Merry Gentlemen," which was recorded by Canadian superstars Barenaked Ladies and Sarah McLachlan. The band sounds like they're busking, as they incorporate a strutting bass line, upbeat acoustic instruments, and occasional bursts of multi-part harmonies. McLachlan, meanwhile, adds new dimensions to the song by layering on a gorgeous, yearning version of "We Three Kings" over the stripped-back music. The song then turns back to "God Rest Ye Merry Gentlemen" at the end, allowing McLachlan and Barenaked Ladies to come together and trade off lines in a vocal-round format.

Like many traditional carols, "God Rest Ye Merry Gentlemen" has a fascinating evolution with many twists and turns. For starters, the song's name is rendered as "God rest you merry, gentlemen"—a commonly accepted variation—in W. B. Sandys' 1833 book *Christmas Carols, Ancient and Modern*. Scholars further point out that the Oxford English Dictionary notes the phrase "God rest you merry" has been used since 1534 and means "God grant you peace and happiness," while Shakespeare also includes the phrase in *As You Like It*.

However, the song has had different names at various junctures. In a manuscript dating from circa 1650, the carol has recognizable lyrics but is titled "Sit you merry gentlemen." When published in 1760 as part of a single sheet verse called "Three new Christmas carols," it was called "God rest on merry, gentlemen." And in a 19th-century collection of traditional English ballads and songs called The *Roxburghe Ballads*, the song is referenced as "God Rest You, Merry Gentlemen."

Countless Christian and secular artists have covered "God Rest Ye Merry Gentlemen" over the years, although the Barenaked Ladies and McLachlan version was one of the most successful. In 2014, the tune reached No. 22 on *Billboard*'s Holiday Digital Song Sales chart.

O HOLY NIGHT

2002 · JOSH GROBAN

Songwriters: Placide Cappeau (original lyrics); Adolphe-Charles Adam (music); John Sullivan Dwight (English translation)
Also covered by: Mariah Carey, Celine Dion, Martina McBride

NOBODY WILL EVER top the Christmas crooning triumvirate of Bing Crosby, Perry Como, and Frank Sinatra. But in contemporary times, another trio of formidable voices—Andrea Bocelli, Josh Groban, and Michael Bublé—are certainly picking up the slack.

Los Angeles native Groban brings an operatic and dramatic vibe to a 2002 version of "O Holy Night," which was one of his first major chart hits. As piano and an orchestra sweep gracefully in the background, he earnestly sings the lyrics—which celebrate the holiness and salvation associated with the birth of Jesus Christ—and builds to a big finish, full of vibrato-laden high notes.

The origins of "O Holy Night" date back to France in the mid-1800s. A wine merchant and poet named Placide Cappeau wrote words at the behest of a church in Roquemaure, celebrating new stained-glass windows. Adolphe-Charles Adam—a composer known for ballets and operas—then composed music for Cappeau's words, creating a carol known as *"Cantique de Noël"* ("Song of Christmas") or *"Minuit, Chrétiens"* ("Midnight, Christians"). In 1847, a woman named Emily Laurey sang this new song for the first time at Roquemaure's Christmas midnight mass.

Despite its religious story line, "O Holy Night" soon caused controversy. Adam was Jewish and Cappeau's politics soon took a socialist turn. Neither of these revelations pleased French Catholics, who no longer embraced the song. However, several years after this controversy, an American minister named John Sullivan Dwight caught wind of the carol and translated the song into English, ensuring its longevity.

Interestingly enough, "O Holy Night" is also notable for the role it played in several other social and cultural movements. According to *Relevant* magazine, the song "became a favorite of Christian abolitionists" thanks to lyrical references to human equality and breaking free from oppression. (Unsurprisingly, Dwight was also an abolitionist.) A few decades later, "O Holy Night" also had the distinction of being the first song ever played on the radio, as a man named Reginald Fessenden played the tune on violin during a Christmas Eve broadcast from Massachusetts.

Taken from 2002's *Josh Groban in Concert*, Groban's version of "O Holy Night" reached No. 1 on *Billboard*'s Adult Contemporary chart—a position the crooner would later reach once again with takes on other Christmas songs, like "I'll Be Home for Christmas" and "Have Yourself a Merry Little Christmas."

CANDY CANE CHILDREN

2002 • WHITE STRIPES

Songwriter: Jack White

THE WHITE STRIPES were probably destined to release a Christmas song. After all, the Detroit duo—vocalist/guitarist Jack White and drummer Meg White—already *looked* like candy canes while playing, because they favored color-coordinated red-and-white outfits as stage wear. For good measure, a publishing company linked to the band was also sweetly named Peppermint Stripe Music.

According to lore (and the Urban Dictionary), White Stripes mega-fans are also known as "Candy Cane Children." That fanciful phrase happens to be the name of the band's original Christmas single, which first appeared in 1998 on the *Surprise*

Package Volume 2 compilation and was later reissued on the 2002 seven-inch *Merry Christmas from . . . The White Stripes.*

"Candy Cane Children" isn't necessarily a jaunty holiday single, however. Musically, it's a garage-rock dirge, driven by Jack White's bluesy guitar acrobatics—including a rickety, evocative solo—and Meg White's ominous stomp grooves. Lyrically, it's even more unsettling, with references to a candy cane boy and a candy cane girl who both seem out of sorts and isolated—and perhaps even in the headspace to do something serious (or violent) they might regret. However, White's lyrics warn the children to hang on until Christmas and to think before they act.

"Candy Cane Children" grew into one of the White Stripes' most beloved non-album tracks and has appeared in multiple special editions or compilations. That includes being packaged in a White Stripes–themed Christmas 2010 boxed set, *The White Stripes Vinyl Starter Merchandise Collection*, alongside headphones and a portable record player; pressed as a three-inch vinyl single as part of a 2019 Record Store Day release for the label Third Man Records; and included on the soundtrack of a 2020 White Stripes–branded online yule log video.

CHRISTMAS TIME (DON'T LET THE BELLS END)

2003 • THE DARKNESS

Songwriters: Ed Graham, Dan Hawkins, Justin Hawkins, Frankie Poullain

FEW BANDS ARE as over the top as UK glam rock band the Darkness. Fittingly, the group's first holiday song, "Christmas Time (Don't Let the Bells End)," is a flamboyant power ballad in the vein of Queen or Electric Light Orchestra. Frontman Justin Hawkins uses the very top of his falsetto vocal range to let out epic shrieks and squeals, as majestic heavy-metal guitars and a shower of twinkling sleigh bell–augmented percussion explode around him. As the song nears its end, a stacked vocal choir enters the fray, creating the perfect atmosphere for a crowd sing-along.

Lyrically, "Christmas Time (Don't Let the Bells End)" tells a slightly different (and less upbeat) story. Things start off lighthearted, with references to mulled wine and pretending to like terrible presents, as well as several lyrical double entendres hinting at crude slang terms. However, "Christmas Time (Don't Let the Bells End)" then turns melancholy: The narrator frets about a relationship that seems to be on shaky ground—they're alone under the mistletoe, for example—and pleads for it to endure.

"Christmas Time (Don't Let the Bells End)" peaked at No. 2 in the UK, losing out on the coveted No. 1 Christmas single slot to a cover of Tears for Fears' "Mad World" by Gary Jules and Michael Andrews. It also later appeared on a reissue of the band's debut album, *Permission to Land*.

In a 2022 episode of his YouTube blog, Hawkins joked that "Christmas Time (Don't Let the Bells End)" continues to impact the band's trajectory all these years later. "I'd love to step out of a bus and be in 100 degrees searing heat," he said. "That would be astounding. We always tour in the winter because we got a Christmas song." Hawkins then lightly recommended that younger bands write a "summer smash instead" because "the touring's much more fun."

Make no mistake, however: Hawkins loves playing "Christmas Time (Don't Let the Bells End)" live. In a 2019 interview with *Shortlist*, he called their holiday-time live performances of the song "a moment of genuine euphoria" and added, "It's a great moment for us as a band, and I think everybody in the room enjoys it. It's Christmas time, and everyone's singing—that's what it's all about, isn't it?"

THE FIRST NOEL

2003 · WHITNEY HOUSTON

Songwriter: Traditional
Also covered by: Gabby Barrett, Mariah Carey, the *Glee* cast, Carrie Underwood

HOLIDAY MUSIC is one genre where the secular and religious intermingle. Part of that is because the Christian genesis of Christmas (the birth of Jesus Christ) is seamlessly incorporated into all aspects of the holiday. However, many artists grew up singing in church—and grew up singing Christmas-related hymns in church—meaning they are predisposed to covering religious songs.

Whitney Houston is one of those artists: Before she was even a teenager, she was a soloist in the junior gospel choir at a Baptist church. Unsurprisingly, this background informs her 2003 full-length *One Wish: The Holiday Album* and, specifically, the album-opening rendition of "The First Noel." A low-lit R&B slow jam with finger-snap beats, sparkling keyboards, and burbling piano, the song finds her alternating between a smoky lower range and drawing on her gospel experience to infuse the music with lovely spiritual overtones. She trills high notes and gives special vocal emphasis to Jesus and references to his birth, meaning the song sounds like the centerpiece of a church service.

According to the Online Etymology Dictionary, the word *noel* itself has roots in the late 14th century—specifically the words *nowel* or *nouel* (which means "Christmas, the Feast of the Nativity") that's derived from an Old French word *noel* that means "the Christmas season." "The First Noel" is a traditional English Christmas carol, although experts aren't 100 percent sure as to when the song originally dates from. However, like many carols, it's evolved across the centuries.

"The First Noel" is rendered as "The First Nowel That the Angel Did Say" in the 1823 Davies Gilbert collection *Some Ancient Christmas Carols*. However, the song's called "The First Nowell" in the Roud Folk Song Index, a collection that tracks English language songs passed down through history, and in several seminal publications: W. B. Sandys' 1833 collection *Christmas Carols, Ancient and Modern* and 1871's *Christmas Carols New and Old*, edited by John Stainer and Henry Ramsden Bramley.

Regardless, the theme of "The First Noel"—describing the scenes that led up to the birth of Jesus Christ—shine through, no matter what version you're reading. The song's title translates, roughly, as "The First Christmas"—meaning plenty of references to the Three Wise Men and a bright guiding star leading to the birth of a future king. Over the years, "The First Noel" has been covered by country, pop, and Christian artists, ensuring that this timeless and holy song reaches new generations.

A GREAT BIG SLED

2006 • THE KILLERS

Songwriters: Brandon Flowers, Dave Keuning,
Mark Stoermer, Ronnie Vannucci Jr.

CHARITY SINGLES didn't fall by the wayside after the 1980s. In fact, artists making music as a way to give back only seemed to become more popular in the subsequent decades. For example, during the 1990s, the socially conscious alternative rock boom led to an abundance of benefit compilations recorded for various organizations and causes.

That trend continued into the 2000s and beyond—including, notably, when Las Vegas synth-rock band the Killers recorded "A Great Big Sled" in 2006 to benefit the then-new (RED) initiative. Cofounded by U2 lead singer Bono, (RED) was formed to raise money to fight diseases such as malaria, tuberculosis, and HIV/AIDS. "The best way for us to help is to do something that we are actually good at," Killers guitarist Dave Keuning told the *Independent (UK)*. "And that's writing songs."

The Killers wrote "A Great Big Sled" while on tour in the UK, specifically during

a sound check. "We often use our sound checks to write new material, as they're the perfect time to spend half an hour noodling away," Keuning continued, "and Brandon [Flowers, the Killers' frontman] and I decided that it would be great to do a Christmas song." Written from the perspective of an adult longing for a more innocent holiday time, Flowers's lyrics recall the days when girls and boys didn't need to worry about much but playing in the snow and having peaceful dreams. In the song's chorus, Flowers recounts one of those dreams: yearning for an opportunity to hop on the titular large sled and be Santa Claus.

"A Great Big Sled" came together quickly. On a day off, the Killers headed to a recording studio owned by ex–Dire Straits leader Mark Knopfler with Alan Moulder; the latter had mixing credits on the Killers' 2004 debut *Hot Fuss* and also co-produced the band's 2006 album *Sam's Town*. Aware of the high bar set by so many holiday songs, the band members were determined to record a Christmas rock song that was classic and timeless. "I was trying to think what the Flaming Lips would do if they wrote a Christmas song, and that's what we got," Flowers later told *NME*. "What's funny is that it sounds nothing like the Flaming Lips."

He's not wrong: While "A Great Big Sled" does contain plenty of the whimsical percussion favored by the Flaming Lips, the midtempo song is very much in the vein of the keyboard-speckled Americana rock the Killers favored at the time. Airy synths and chugging, chiming guitars dominate, with the occasional keyboard squeal for color, matching the keening vibe of Flowers' voice. For good measure, Moulder's wife Toni Halliday, who fronted the noisy shoegaze band Curve, contributed vocals. Her melodic, dusky presence adds nostalgia and whimsy to the song, as she muses about the magic of Christmas sounds.

"A Great Big Sled" ended up performing modestly well, reaching No. 11 on the UK Official Download chart and peaking at No. 54 on the *Billboard* Hot 100. However, the single ended up inspiring the Killers to record a string of holiday singles, which ended up being compiled on 2011's *(Red) Christmas* EP.

CHRISTMAS TREE

2008 • LADY GAGA

Songwriters: Lady Gaga and Space Cowboy

LADY GAGA had much to celebrate in 2008. The over-the-top pop star released her debut album, *The Fame*; opened New Kids on the Block's reunion tour; and was nominated for a Grammy Award for Best Dance Recording for the upbeat EDM tune "Just Dance."

For the (tree) topper, she also wrote and recorded a holiday song, "Christmas Tree." Although the kicky electro-pop song samples "Deck the Halls" and makes a passing reference to "Little Drummer Boy," it's not remotely traditional. Thematically, the song is arch and eyebrow-raising—in short, very reminiscent of Gaga's lyrical style during this time. The tune refers to nudity and incorporates sexual double entendres, painting a picture of a rather risqué holiday.

Gaga wrote "Christmas Tree" with the British-raised musician and producer Space Cowboy (real name: Nicolas Jean-Pierre Dresti). "Nobody knew who she was, she was just starting up, and we spoke on the phone, we got on really, really well—it was amazing!" he told *Urb* in 2009. "We figured out that we shared pretty much the same experiences; we'd been doing similar things on opposite sides of the Atlantic." The pair ended up collaborating not just on "Christmas Tree" but also on a glittery electro song called "Starstruck" that ended up on *The Fame*. Space Cowboy walked away from the experience impressed. "She's super-creative, she's amazing—the best writer I'd ever seen, and [the] best performer."

Co-production, meanwhile, came from Space Cowboy and Martin Kierszenbaum. The latter, who worked in A&R at Interscope Records and founded Gaga's label, Cherrytree Records, was another frequent Gaga collaborator around this time. (When she makes a reference to "Cherry Cherry Boom Boom" at the end of the song, she's affectionately referencing one of his nicknames.) Kierszenbaum was no stranger to pop music success—he co-wrote t.A.T.u.'s "All the Things She Said"—and his approach gave "Christmas Tree" an edgy sheen. In fact, it's the rare holiday song that could get a club dance floor moving and grooving. Gaga shows off both her brassy, melodic vocal acumen and speak-sing, robotic side—a combination that would soon propel her to superstardom.

"Christmas Tree" was released the week before Christmas in 2008 and would later sell well enough to reach the top 25 of *Billboard*'s digital holiday songs chart a few years later, as well as appear on multiple Christmas compilations around the world.

MUST BE SANTA

2009 • BOB DYLAN

Songwriters: Hal Moore and Bill Fredericks
Also covered by: Brave Combo, Mitch Miller, She & Him

BOB DYLAN'S sense of humor is often overshadowed by his reputation as a serious bard. But he'll occasionally burst into joking stage banter during concerts, and his lyrical wordplay is often more playful and rakish than it appears. He's also a far more accomplished actor than you might think, both in drama and comedy. In fact, Dylan's perhaps never been funnier than he was in the video for his 2009 holiday song "Must Be Santa."

Wearing (alternately) a white and black top hat with a long-haired wig, Dylan is the quiet ringleader of a massive holiday rager, inciting mischief as people swing

on chandeliers, dance to upbeat music, and get warm and toasty on alcoholic beverages. He's not in the middle of the mayhem, mind you; instead, he's impishly egging on the proceedings in the background.

The raucous party atmosphere matches the vibe of "Must Be Santa," which appears on Dylan's first-ever Christmas album, *Christmas in the Heart*. (Appropriately enough, he produced it himself under the very wintry moniker Jack Frost, a favored pseudonym.) Co-written by Hal Moore and Bill Fredericks, "Must Be Santa" is based on a German drinking song called "*Schnitzelbank*." The rowdy tune describes elements of Santa's look and persona—a beard, his hearty laugh, a ruddy nose, a red suit, boots—and contorts these adjectives into tongue-twisting descriptors that build and build as the song progresses. Throw in references to US presidents and Santa's reindeer and it's a recipe for absurdity.

The first major rendition of "Must Be Santa" came from noted producer and musician Mitch Miller, who hosted the TV sensation *Sing Along with Mitch*. A 1960 *Billboard* review of Miller's take on the song (which was backed by the B-side "Christmas Spirit") noted that he and "his gang of sing-alongers come [through] with a pair of sprightly holiday-styled sides" that "grab plenty of yule activity." In a 2009 interview, Dylan said he first encountered "Must Be Santa" via Miller's version. "But this version [I did] comes from a band called Brave Combo," he explained. "They're a regional band out of Texas that takes regular songs and changes the way you think about them."

Dylan's polka- and klezmer-influenced version of "Must Be Santa" is indeed faithful to Brave Combo's brisk and loose cover. Structured like a call-and-response between him and a choir of voices, the song is theatrical and upbeat. Dylan and his band members—which at the time included musicians like bassist Tony Garnier and drummer George Receli, as well as guest accordionist David Hidalgo of Los Lobos—toss together music that whirls around as quickly as a spinning top. Unlike in the video, however, Dylan takes center stage within this dizzying bacchanalia—singing in a raspy, lively voice, and putting his own stamp on Christmas cheer.

MISTLETOE

2011 • JUSTIN BIEBER

Songwriters: Nasri Atweh, Justin Bieber, Adam Messinger

FOR POP STARS looking to bring joy to fans, releasing a Christmas album is just about a foolproof solution. Holiday covers allow musicians to show off their sweet and sentimental side, while putting their stamp on some of history's most timeless tunes. Recording originals, meanwhile, gives these artists cred and helps position them as a permanent part of the holiday pop canon.

Justin Bieber certainly swung for the fences with his first Christmas album, 2011's *Under the Mistletoe*: He duetted with Mariah Carey on what was dubbed the "SuperFestive!" version of her mega-smash "All I Want for Christmas Is You," and also included collaborations with Busta Rhymes, Usher, and Boyz II Men. In 2011, Bieber told MTV News he decided to make a Christmas album as a gift of sorts to fans, since it had been a while since he released a full-length album. (His debut, *My World*, was issued and reissued in various configurations starting in 2009.)

A laid-back, reggae-tinged original song, called "Mistletoe," ended up being the album's lead single. "We are in the holiday spirit," he added. "I'm really excited. [The song is] really catchy. I know all my fans are going to love it. It's something that I feel like they're going to be singing every Christmas."

"Mistletoe" deserved such an honor, as it demonstrates why Bieber became a pop superstar at such a young age. He shows off a lovely, soulful, and romantic croon that brings the song's lyrics to life. The smitten protagonist is ditching all the trappings of Christmas—making a list for Santa Claus, hanging with family, enjoying the snow—in favor of parking himself under the mistletoe so he can smooch his beloved. "Mistletoe" offers some clever spins on the usual holiday romance trope (for example, Bieber compares himself finding true love to the Three Wise Men using a star as a guide), which only adds to the song's charm.

It's safe to say that fans were *definitely* hollering "Mistletoe" the year of its release: The tune debuted at No. 11 on the *Billboard* Hot 100 on November 5, 2011—the highest debut position ever for a Christmas song—and ended up reaching the top of the Holiday Songs chart that year. *Under the Mistletoe* also set a chart record: It became the first holiday record from a male artist to debut atop the *Billboard* album charts. Bieber hasn't released another Christmas album to date, although he later performed the Stevie Wonder–popularized "Someday at Christmas" at the White House in 2009 and released a cover of "Rockin' Around the Christmas Tree" in 2020.

IT'S BEGINNING TO LOOK A LOT LIKE CHRISTMAS

2011 • MICHAEL BUBLÉ

Songwriter: Meredith Willson
Also covered by: Harry Connick Jr., Noah Cyrus, Johnny Mathis, Pentatonix

IF MARIAH CAREY is fond of calling herself the Queen of Christmas, then Michael Bublé is the undisputed King of Christmas—and that's not just because he topped *Billboard*'s Adult Contemporary chart with a cover of Carey's signature holiday tune, "All I Want for Christmas Is You." As of 2021, his festive 2011 compilation *Christmas* had sold more than 16 million albums globally and been streamed more than 4 billion times. Overall, Bublé has also charted nearly two dozen different songs on *Billboard*'s Holiday 100, ranging from duets ("White Christmas" with fellow Canadian Shania Twain) to standards ("Let It Snow! Let It Snow! Let It Snow!").

One of his biggest and most enduring holiday hits is his version of "It's Beginning to Look a Lot Like Christmas," which has reached the top 10 on the holiday chart and top 20 on the overall *Billboard* pop charts. In a warm, smooth croon, Bublé runs down the glorious signs of Christmas: stores decorated for the holidays, festive trees, tantalizing toys. Ultimately, however, the song concludes that nothing compares to the decorations in your own home—and the festive song in your soul. Sugar-dusted strings, harp, and piano swirl around like a fluffy snow shower, creating a picturesque (and even cozy) atmosphere.

"It's Beginning to Look a Lot Like Christmas" (which was initially known as "It's Beginning to Look Like Christmas") is the handiwork of Meredith Willson. The Mason City, Iowa, native wrote music and lyrics for the indelible Broadway musical *The Music Man*—for which he won the first-ever Best Original Cast Album (Broadway or TV) Grammy Award—and the equally irrepressible musical *The Unsinkable Molly Brown*, as well as Glenn Miller's 1941 hit, "You and I."

Willson published his festive Christmas tune in 1951, although there is some question about the song's inspiration. Some people believe he wrote it in Canada, at Yarmouth's Grand Hotel, which has a park right across the street. In fact, a bellhop told the *(Halifax, Nova Scotia) Chronicle Herald* in 2011 that he recalled a hotel guest he believed was Willson, lugging a steamer trunk and visiting to write. However, other people contend that the song's references point to Mason City, which also features a tranquil park across from a hotel. At any rate, no one has ever definitively been able to rule out—or rule *in*—either of these scenarios.

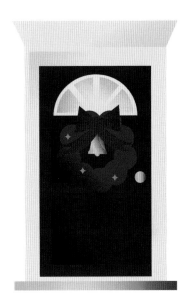

What isn't in question? The immediate success of—and enduring love for—"It's Beginning to Look a Lot Like Christmas." Sixty years before Bublé had a major hit with the tune, a version by Perry Como and the Fontane Sisters with Mitchell Ayres & His Orchestra also became a hit; like Bublé's, it remains a popular holiday season staple. Willson himself also repurposed the song in his 1963 Broadway musical *Here's Love*, which is based on *Miracle on 34th Street.* And in the decades since, pop artists and crooners alike have embraced the song's warm whimsy.

UNDERNEATH THE TREE

2013 • KELLY CLARKSON

Songwriters: Kelly Clarkson and Greg Kurstin

KELLY CLARKSON can sing *anything*. That's evident on her talk show, where in her Kellyoke segment she's covered songs you'd expect her to slay (Trisha Yearwood's "How Do I Live," the Linda Ronstadt–popularized "Blue Bayou") and some completely out-of-left-field choices (multiple Radiohead songs, the Smiths' "How Soon Is Now?").

But for her first Christmas album, 2013's *Wrapped in Red*, Clarkson stuck to the classics, at least stylistically. "Underneath the Tree" is a joyful song about how true love makes Christmas that much better and brighter. Before coupling up, the song's protagonist was lonely and dreaded the holidays; life was like a staticky, black-and-white TV show. After, however, everything dazzles in Technicolor—presents, carolers in the snow—and Christmas is cozy and perfect. In fact, the narrator doesn't need tangible things like gifts; the best present of all is having their honey by their side.

Clarkson wrote the song with Greg Kurstin, who started his career in the quirky band Geggy Tah before diving into production for mainstream pop artists and forming the synth-pop duo the Bird and the Bee. Together, the pair craft music that harkens back to the 1960s Wall of Sound production style: lush instrumentation bursting with saxes and horns; bells and chimes; and twinkling percussion. Clarkson herself turns in a powerful, dynamic vocal performance whose impressive dips and soars rival only those of Darlene Love and Mariah Carey.

Wrapped in Red debuted at No. 3 on the overall *Billboard* 200 pop charts and reached No. 1 on the *Billboard* Top Holiday Albums chart. Unsurprisingly, it was certified gold and platinum in early December 2013. As if that weren't impressive enough, "Underneath the Tree" was a massive global hit. In fact, ASCAP later named the single the No. 1 tune on the Top 10 ASCAP New Classic Holiday Songs of 2021, a list that measures the biggest songs released in the 21st century. In the coming years, Clarkson would parlay this success into many holiday events and appearances—and also later release another Christmas album in 2021, *When Christmas Comes Around . . .* , featuring the cheeky single "Christmas Isn't Canceled (Just You)."

SANTA TELL ME

2014 • ARIANA GRANDE

Songwriters: Ariana Grande, Savan Kotecha, Ilya Salmanzadeh

ARIANA GRANDE loves Christmas. In the music video for "thank u, next," Grande re-creates the Christmas pageant scene from the movie *Mean Girls.* She joined her idol Mariah Carey on the 2020 streaming event *Mariah Carey's Magical Christmas Special* and appeared on a remix of Carey's "Oh Santa!" alongside Jennifer Hudson. For good measure, Grande has also covered some of the greatest holiday songs ever (Wham!'s "Last Christmas") and released multiple holiday EPs, including 2015's *Christmas & Chill.*

You might say that Grande's affection for Christmas started with 2014's "Santa Tell Me." The narrator of the playful pop/R&B song has one request for Jolly Ol' Saint Nick: to know whether she should waste her time on her current new romance. There's precedent for this—the narrator shares that she once had a dude ditch her between Christmas and New Year's Day—and she just wants to know if he's going to ghost her or stomp on her heart in the coming year. Call it self-preservation—or asking Santa to be a fortune teller and give her a hint as to what's to come.

Grande co-wrote "Santa Tell Me" with frequent collaborators Ilya Salmanzadeh and Savan Kotecha. The songwriters were also involved with her hits "Problem," "God Is a Woman," and "Break Up with Your Girlfriend, I'm Bored," as well as the Ellie Goulding mega-smash "Love Me Like You Do." "Santa Tell Me" is of a piece with these sleek, buoyant pop songs: It boasts finger-snapping percussion, twinkling strings, a gospel choir, and the kind of beats that make you want to dance around your room like a giddy kid.

The song's message and vibe struck a chord with fans around the world. "Santa Tell Me" reached No. 1 on *Billboard*'s Holiday 100 chart in 2015 and has also reached No. 12 on the overall *Billboard* Hot 100, in addition to enjoying chart success around the world. The tune also landed at No. 2 on the Top 10 ASCAP New Classic Holiday Songs of 2021—a list that measures the most popular songs released in the 21st century—trailing only Kelly Clarkson's "Underneath the Tree."

CAROL OF THE BELLS

2014 • PENTATONIX

Songwriters: Mykola Leontovych (music); Peter J. Wilhousky (lyrics)
Also covered by: Lindsey Stirling and Trans-Siberian Orchestra

IF WE'RE TALKING about Christmas vocal groups, few collectives—besides, maybe, the Andrews Sisters—compare to the a cappella act Pentatonix. Formed in 2011 in Arlington, Texas, the troupe rose to prominence after winning the third

season of the NBC music reality show *The Sing-Off.* Among their (many) specialties is holiday music: They've released multiple Christmas albums and embarked on several festive-themed tours, including 2022's Pentatonix: A Christmas Spectacular.

Pentatonix's secret isn't just seamless vocal harmonies and inventive arrangements that include elements like beatboxing. They have a knack for transforming familiar songs into something transcendent. Take their version of "Carol of the Bells," which weaves solemn vocal harmonies and the occasional rhythmic percolation into the familiar bom-bom-bom-bom arpeggiated melodic part. It's reverent enough for a traditional church service but progressive enough to fit in the contemporary secular music scene. Pentatonix's version peaked at No. 66 on *Billboard*'s Holiday 100 chart in 2013.

The history of "Carol of the Bells" starts in Ukraine and a song called "*Shchedryk*," written by composer Mykola Leontovych and first performed by a Kyiv choir in 1916. Leontovych was hired by the choir director Oleksander Koshyts to write a tune based on existing traditional Ukrainian folk songs. According to a 2014 news story, drawing on research from Rice University anthropology graduate student Anthony Potoczniak, "*Shchedryk*" ended up being a "winter well-wishing song" involving a swallow (a bird) sharing good news about a successful coming year. Fittingly, the folk song that served as original source material was popular around New Year's celebrations in Ukraine.

In the ensuing years, things weren't quite so peaceful, as Ukraine faced significant challenges to their sovereignty and culture due to World War I and the Russian Revolution. As Potoczniak characterized it, "*Shchedryk*" emerged "during a time when there was intense political struggle and social upheaval" there. In fact,

Leontovych himself was killed in 1921. "This was a political matter," Valentyna Kuzyk, a senior researcher at the Rylsky Institute of Art, Folklore Studies, and Ethnology in Ukraine, told *Slate* in 2019.

However, "*Shchedryk*" lived on and gained an international audience. During a short period of time in the late 1910s when Ukraine was independent, a troupe called the Ukrainian Republic Capella toured Europe and performed the song. After this choir ceased to exist, Koshyts formed the Ukrainian National Chorus, which toured North America and Europe as a form of cultural exchange. In fact, "Carol of the Bells" premiered in the US to great acclaim at Carnegie Hall on October 5, 1922.

These global travels introduced "*Shchedryk*" to American choir director and arranger Peter Wilhousky, who penned new lyrics and published his own take on the song, now dubbed "Carol of the Bells," in 1936. Perhaps this backstory explains why "Carol of the Bells" is such a moving holiday song that's often interpreted in moody ways. Its origins are both hopeful and somber, yearning and grieving, and long for the comfort of home. In 2022, with Ukraine under attack by Russia and experiencing extreme wartime violence, the yearning undertones of "Carol of the Bells" have sadly never felt more relevant.

SOMEDAY AT CHRISTMAS

2015 • ANDRA DAY & STEVIE WONDER

Songwriters: Ron Miller and Bryan Wells
Also covered by: Pearl Jam, Jack Johnson, Lizzo

STEVIE WONDER loves collaborating with superstars. During a career that's spanned seven decades, he's teamed up with A-list talent such as Whitney Houston, Paul McCartney, Dionne Warwick, Barbra Streisand, and Michael Jackson. As Wonder's career progressed, however, the icon has also made it a point to champion and elevate the profile of talented younger artists like India.Arie, 98 Degrees, and Beyoncé.

One of his more recent protégés is Andra Day, a ferociously talented, Grammy-winning vocalist who slips easily between the soul, blues, pop, and R&B genres. In 2015, Wonder and Day appeared together in an Apple commercial performing a duet of "Someday at Christmas." Wisely, the song's arrangement is sparse: It's just Wonder at the piano doing what he does best, making the instrument sing with his inimitable, intuitive, fluid style.

Vocally, Day and Wonder start off alternating singing lines—although, unsurprisingly, "Someday at Christmas" shines when the musicians join forces and sing together. Their vocal blend is note-perfect, of course, but also incredibly moving, especially since the song has a quietly political theme. Its lyrics are full of calls for peace and equality and long for eradicating hunger and the violence of war. Like many other Wonder songs, however, the tone is optimistic and hopeful; "Someday at Christmas" believes better days are possible in the future.

Initially the title track of Wonder's 1967 holiday album, *Someday at Christmas*, the song was written by Ron Miller and Bryan Wells. Miller was an especially productive Motown Records writer who would also later compose lyrics to

Wonder's 1968 hit "For Once in My Life." Along with Wells, he also co-wrote multiple Wonder songs, such as "A Place in the Sun" and "Yester-Me, Yester-You, Yesterday."

When "Someday at Christmas" was released initially, its subject matter reflected the burgeoning late-1960s civil rights and antiwar movements and protests against racial oppression. Decades later, "Someday at Christmas" has lost none of its power. (For proof, look no further than a 2022 cover by Lizzo that reached the top 10 in the UK.) In fact, Day had nothing but positive things to say about her time recording with Wonder. As for what she learned from the collaboration, she praised the icon's "passion," among other things. "We'll be sitting there working, recording, and he'll take time to start playing around on the piano or harpejji or on anything," she said. "And he's just a master of all of them. But he still has that musician's drive to play and touch whatever is around him."

CHRISTMAS TREE FARM

2019 • TAYLOR SWIFT

Songwriter: Taylor Swift

TAYLOR SWIFT excels at incorporating elements of her own life into her songwriting: bad boyfriends, painful breakups, and fairy-tale romances. However, few Swift tunes are as on the nose as 2019's "Christmas Tree Farm." For starters, the song's music video features home movies of Swift taken throughout the years at Christmas, including the time when she received an acoustic guitar as a gift.

If that wasn't perfect enough—the pop superstar also grew up on an actual

Christmas tree farm in rural Pennsylvania. "I had the most magical childhood, running free and going anywhere I wanted to in my head," Swift once told *Rolling Stone*. That whimsical, fantasy-rich vibe naturally permeates "Christmas Tree Farm." In a behind-the-scenes video on creating the song, she shared insights into the song's lyrics: "It's about how you're in the city and you're stressed out and your life is feeling low, but in your heart is a Christmas tree farm."

In other words, this farm is both an actual place where people can go to grab a tree and enjoy festive events—and also a figurative happy place that represents safety, coziness, and fun. When you go to a Christmas tree farm, your worries and cares melt away; it's the platonic ideal of seasonal joy.

"Christmas Tree Farm" wasn't Swift's first holiday single. In 2007, she issued *The Taylor Swift Holiday Collection*, which featured versions of Wham!'s "Last Christmas" and Eartha Kitt's "Santa Baby" as well as two originals. However, these songs came out when Swift was still firmly a country music artist. "Christmas Tree Farm," meanwhile, represented her sound and approach as a confident, chameleonic pop superstar. Swift belts out the lyrics earnestly as warm piano chords and sleigh bells shimmer and chime around her. It's the sonic equivalent of sipping hot cocoa while blasting holiday music and baking cookies with people you love—a perfect, loving memory that brings a smile during tough times.

Proving that perfection *can* be improved upon, Swift released another version of the song, "Christmas Tree Farm (Old Timey Version)," in 2021. This variation featured orchestral accompaniment, turning the already traditional tune into a cozy, jazzier number. "It feels like it's that more laid-back Christmas feel, of doing all your shopping and relaxing by a fire," Swift said. "It's definitely a little bit more of that old-school Christmas song feel."

Acknowledgments

I have loved Christmas music my entire life, and so writing a book about this topic is a dream come true. Thanks to my editor, Jordana Hawkins, book designer Joanna Price, associate art director Katie Benezra, illustrator Darling Clementine, publisher Kristin Kiser, publicist Seta Zink, copyeditor and proofreader Diana Drew, and everyone at Running Press for their care, diligence, and support in shepherding this book to publication.

Sources

All artist names and song titles found via the original artwork published at Discogs (discogs.com). Chart positions verified via *Billboard* issues published at World Radio History (worldradiohistory.com) and UK charts found at Official Album Charts (officialcharts.com). Other information verified at the Internet Movie Database (imdb.com), The Guinness World Records website (guinnessworldrecords. com), lyrics sites (genius.com), and via YouTube (youtube.com) and the streaming platform Apple Music.

Traditional, "12 Days of Christmas"

Austin, Frederic (arr.). "The Twelve Days of Christmas (Traditional Song)," London: Novello, 1909.

"New Music: Songs and Instrumental Pieces." *Manchester Courier and Lancashire General Advertiser* (England), December 18, 1909.

"Sir Herbert Marshall's Concert." *Leicester Chronicle and Leicestershire Mercury* (England), December 18, 1909.

Pai, Tanya. "The 12 Days of Christmas: The Story Behind the Holiday's Most Annoying Carol." Vox, updated December 1, 2022.

Bing Crosby, "White Christmas"

Carroll, Harrison. "Bing Crosby Is Rushing Yule Recording to London." *Charlotte Observer* (Charlotte, North Carolina), December 16, 1941.

Cogan, Jim; Clark, William. *Temples of Sound: Inside the Great Recording Studios*. San Francisco: Chronicle Books, 2003.

Harris, Roy J., Jr. "The Best-Selling Record of All: 'White Christmas' and the Reasons It Endures." *Wall Street Journal*, December 5, 2009.

Lost Media Wiki (archive). "White Christmas (found recording of original radio performance of song; 1941)." lostmediawiki.com.

Ober Peak, Mayme. "Berlin, Producer Develop an Idea into Musical Film." *Buffalo Evening News* (Buffalo, New York), December 13, 1941.

Rosen, Jody. *White Christmas: The Story of an American Song*. New York: Scribner, 2002.

Special News Service. "Irving Berlin's Idea May Be Whiz, But It Sounds Complex." *Spokesman-Review* (Spokane, Washington), October 5, 1941.

Bing Crosby, "I'll Be Home for Christmas"

Library of Congress, "I'll Be Home for Christmas" (song collection). Found at: https://loc.gov/item/ihas.200000010.

"'Home for Christmas' Pub Dispute Settled." *Billboard*, October 23, 1943.

"Marks Claims 2d 'Home for Xmas' Lift of Its Song." *Billboard*, October 9, 1943.

Weinbender, Nathan. "75 Years after Its Premiere, Bing Crosby's 'White Christmas' Still Enthralls Listeners." *Spokesman-Review* (Spokane, Washington), December 22, 2016.

Judy Garland,
"Have Yourself a Merry Little Christmas"
Bianculli, David. "The Story Behind 'Have Yourself a Merry Little Christmas,'" NPR Fresh Air, November 19, 2010.
Ferguson, John. "Lost Ralph Blane Items Discovered at BACP." *Tulsa World* (Oklahoma), January 23, 2014.

Nat King Cole, "The Christmas Song"
Tormé, Mel. *It Wasn't All Velvet: An Autobiography.* New York: Zebra Books, 1990.

Frank Sinatra, "Jingle Bells"
Masterson, Sam. "Frank Sinatra's 'Jingle Bells' Was Arranged by Music Prodigy from Webster Groves." KMOX, December 22, 2021.
Pierpont, James. "'The One Horse Open Sleigh.'" Sheet music, September 16, 1857. Found at Library of Congress, Music for the Nation: American Sheet Music, 1820–1860.
Strauss, Valerie. "'Jingle Bells'—written for Thanksgiving?" *Washington Post*, December 24, 2013.
Unitarian Universalist Church of Savannah website, www.uusavannah.org.
Willcox, Kris. "James Lord Pierpont and the Mystery of 'Jingle Bells.'" *UUWorld*, December 15, 2014.

Gene Autry, "Here Comes Santa Claus
(Down Santa Claus Lane)"
Cusic, Don. *Gene Autry: His Life and Career.* Jefferson, North Carolina: McFarland, Incorporated, 2007.
Ibid. *The Cowboy in Country Music: An Historical Survey with Artist Profiles.* Jefferson, North Carolina: McFarland, Incorporated, 2011.
Ina Autry (Biography). Accessed via geneautry.com.

Gene Autry, "Rudolph, the Red-Nosed Reindeer"
May, Robert L., as told to Alfred Balk. "How Rudolph Came to Christmas." *Racine Journal-Times Sunday Bulletin* (Racine, Wisconsin), December 22, 1963.
"The Pinafores, Gene Autry's Singing Girl Friends Are Descendants of Pioneer Colorado Ranchers." *Sherbrooke Telegram* (Quebec, Canada), February 9, 1950.
Rumore, Kori. "Rudolph the Red-Nosed Reindeer was created in Chicago by Montgomery Ward Copywriter Robert L. May to Sell Toys in 1939. Here's How the Popular Christmas Character—and Its Author—Went Down in History." *Chicago Tribune*, December 24, 2021.

Ella Fitzgerald & Louis Jordan,
"Baby, It's Cold Outside"
"Party Song." *Time*, June 27, 1949.
Siemaszko, Corky. "Daughter of 'Baby, It's Cold Outside' Writer Frank Loesser Blames Bill Cosby for Recent Radio Bans." NBC News, December 6, 2018.
Yasharoff, Hannah. "More Radio Stations Ban 'Baby It's Cold Outside' Amid #MeToo Controversy." *USA Today*, December 5, 2018.

Bing Crosby & the Andrews Sisters,
"Mele Kalikimaka (Merry Christmas)"
Discography of American Historical Recordings. "Decca Matrix L 5830. Mele Kalikimaka / The Andrews Sisters; Bing Crosby." Accessed via https://adp.library.ucsb.edu.
Hawaiian Music Hall of Fame, "R. Alex Anderson." Accessed via hmhof.org.
Interview, "R. Alex Anderson-Mele Kalikimaka." Accessed via youtube.com/watch?v=6FvMXys3Ffw. 1994.
Kealamakia, Spencer. "5 Versions of 'Mele Kalikimaka' That Beat Bing Crosby's." *Hawaii Magazine*, December 19, 2016.

Jimmy Durante, "Frosty the Snowman"
"Jimmy Durante, Frosty the Snow Man–Review." *Billboard*, December 2, 1950.

Rosemary Clooney, "Suzy Snowflake"
"Rosemary Clooney, Suzy Snowflake–Review." *Billboard*, October 20, 1951.

"The Songwriting Team of Sid Tepper and Roy C. Bennett." Accessed via tepper-bennett.com.

Eartha Kitt, "Santa Baby"

Hond, Paul. "'Santa Baby' Changed My Life." *Columbia Magazine*, December 17, 2020.

Roberts, Randall. "'Santa Baby' Composer Phil Springer, 91, Still Can't Figure Out Why His Sexy Christmas Song Endures." *Los Angeles Times*, December 22, 2017.

Wilson, Earl. "N.Y. Snobbery Can't Faze Him." *Los Angeles Daily News*, December 8, 1953.

Gayla Peevey, "I Want a Hippopotamus for Christmas"

"Local Song Writer Dies." *Winterset Madisonian* (Winterset, Iowa), August 14, 1957.

Scott, Vernon. "Gayla Peevey Really Prefers Oklahoma." *Tribune* (San Luis Obispo, California), August 20, 1953.

Siegel, Robert. "For the Oklahoma City Zoo, Hippos Are a Christmas Tradition." NPR's *All Things Considered*, December 13, 2017.

UP, "Girl's Hit Song Pays Off: She'll Get a Hippo for Christmas." *Press and Sun-Bulletin* (Binghamton, New York), December 12, 1953.

UP, "Little Gayla Peevey Receives Her Hippo." *Alabama Journal* (Montgomery, Alabama), December 24, 1953.

Bobby Helms, "Jingle Bell Rock"

Aamidor, Abe. "Jingle Bell Rocker Gives Pupils a Blast from the Past at Dance." *Indianapolis Star*, December 12, 1992.

Fitzgerald, Jim. "Jim Fitzgerald's Platter Patter." *Evening Express* (Portland, Maine), December 12, 1957.

Stuart, Devan. "No Jingle in His Pockets." *Jacksonville (Florida) Business Journal*, August 27, 2001.

Trust, Gary. "Mariah Carey's 'Christmas' Climbs to No. 3 on Billboard Hot 100, Ariana Grande's 'Next' Leads for Seventh Week." *Billboard*, December 31, 2018.

Elvis Presley, "Blue Christmas"

"Christmas Classics Person of the Day: Billy Hayes III." Accessed via christmasclassics.com.

"HISTORICALLY SPEAKING: 'Blue Christmas' Composer Has Connecticut Connections." *Bulletin* (Norwich, Connecticut), December 7, 2014.

Keith Flynn's Elvis Presley Page. Recording Sessions. Accessed via keithflynn.com.

Chuck Berry, "Run Rudolph Run"

Berry, Chuck. *Chuck Berry: The Autobiography*. New York: Harmony Books, 1987.

Chuck Berry chart positions. Accessed via chuckberry.com.

The Chuck Berry Collectors Blog. "Run! Rudolph, the Red-Nosed Reindeer—and the Copyright Mystery." Accessed via crif.de/ChuckBerry/blog/.

"Chuck Berry, Run, Rudolph, Run" (Review). *Billboard*, December 1, 1958.

The Chipmunks with David Seville, "The Chipmunk Song"

"'Chipmunk' a Yuletide Skyrocket." *Billboard*, December 15, 1958.

Cox, Stephen. "'The Chipmunk Song' Turns 60: Secrets of a Holiday Novelty Smash." *Hollywood Reporter*, December 21, 2018.

Dougherty, Steve. "Squeak of Success." *People*, February 22, 1993.

"Lightning Can Strike Twice." *Billboard*, December 1, 1958.

Rolontz, Bob. "Heavy Action Keys Renaissance of Christmas Singles." *Billboard*, December 22, 1958.

Brenda Lee, "Rockin' Around the Christmas Tree"

Thanki, Juli. "'Rockin' Around the Christmas Tree' Singer Brenda Lee on the Song's Origin and Legacy." *Tennessean*, December 9, 2019.

Dean Martin, "Let It Snow! Let It Snow! Let It Snow!"

Cahn, Sammy. *Sammy Cahn's Rhyming Dictionary*. New York: Cherry Lane Music, 1989.

The Beach Boys, "Little Saint Nick"

Associated Press. "Beach Boys' Love Wins Suit." *Star-Gazette* (Elmira, New York), December 13, 1994.

Bellagio 10452—A Beach Boys Reference site.

1963 day-by-day guide. Accessed via bellagio10452.com.

Murphy, James B. *Becoming the Beach Boys, 1961–1963*. Jefferson, North Carolina: McFarland & Company, 2015.

Darlene Love,

"Christmas (Baby Please Come Home)"

Cher, tweet. "Phil Spector's Xmas Album. Sonny & I Sang on Every Cut. You Can Hear Me." December 16, 2019. Accessed via twitter.com/cher/status/1206463201237512192.

Music Is My Life Podcast. "Darlene Love on Phil Spector, Elvis, *20 Feet from Stardom*." Episode 26, 2019. Accessed via youtube.com/watch?v=hEAD03adAGg.

The Ronettes, "Sleigh Ride"

Lynch, Joe. "Ronnie Spector's Pure-as-Snow Love for Christmas Will Warm Your Heart." *Billboard*, December 12, 2019.

Wind Band Literature. "Sleigh Ride by Leroy Anderson." December 14, 2020. Accessed via windliterature.org.

Vince Guaraldi Trio, "Christmas Time Is Here"

Wernick, Adam, and Ben Manilla. "The Music of Vince Guaraldi Helped Make 'A Charlie Brown Christmas' a Cultural Icon." Studio 360, December 27, 2014.

Andy Williams,

"It's the Most Wonderful Time of the Year"

Herman, Karen. "Interview—Andy Williams." The Television Academy Foundation, September 19, 2005. Accessed via interviews.televisionacademy.com/interviews/andy-williams.

Burl Ives, "A Holly Jolly Christmas"

"Christmas Comes Early to Television This Year." *Hartford Courant* (Connecticut), November 29, 1964.

Thurl Ravenscroft,

"You're a Mean One, Mr. Grinch"

Simpson, Tess. "Daughter of Voice Actor Reflects on Legacy." News Talk 94.1. December 20, 2018.

The Beatles, "Christmas Time (Is Here Again)"

The Beatles Bible. "Recording, Mixing: Christmas Time (Is Here Again)." Accessed via www.beatlesbible.com.

Stevie Wonder, "What Christmas Means to Me"

"Best-Selling Christmas Singles." *Billboard*, December 24, 1966.

James Brown,

"Santa Claus Go Straight to the Ghetto"

Barbee, Bobbie. "Brown Plays Santa to Needy." *Jet* magazine, December 26, 1968.

Davis, David. "Olympic Athletes Who Took a Stand." *Smithsonian*, August 2008.

The Temptations, "Silent Night"

Daley, Jason. "A Brief History of 'Silent Night.'" *Smithsonian*, December 17, 2018.

Malathronas, John. "Skulls, Salt and Snow: 200 Years of 'Silent Night.'" December 14, 2018.

The Carpenters, "Merry Christmas, Darling"

Erickson, Randy. "Pooler's Song Dashed off for a Girl Became a Christmas Standard." *La Crosse Tribune* (La Crosse, Wisconsin), December 23, 2005.

The Carpenters: A Christmas Portrait, TV special. 1978. Accessed via youtube.com/watch?v=Rzaxs_QD5TU.

José Feliciano, "Feliz Navidad"

Del Barco, Mandalit. "50 Years Later, 'Feliz Navidad' Still Delivers on Its Bilingual Message." NPR, December 14, 2020.

Pugh, Jamia. "José Feliciano Celebrates 50 Years of 'Feliz Navidad.'" Associated Press, November 19, 2020.

Runnells, Charles. "50 Years of 'Feliz Navidad': Fun Facts about José Feliciano's Holiday Hit, Livestream Concert." *Fort Myers News-Press* (Florida), December 17, 2020.

Donny Hathaway, "This Christmas"

Borrelli, Christopher. "'This Christmas': How a Chicago Postal Worker and Donny Hathaway Created a Holiday Classic." *Chicago Tribune*, December 20, 2017.

Hoekstra, David. "Donny Hathaway's 'This

Christmas.'" *Chicago Sun-Times*, December 24, 2012.

The Jackson 5, "Santa Claus Is Comin' to Town"

Collins, Ace. *Stories Behind the Greatest Hits of Christmas*. Grand Rapids, Michigan: Zondervan, 2010.

Matos, Marimer. "Family Wants Rights Back to 'Santa Claus' Song." *Courthouse News*, December 20, 2011.

Sanders, Jacquin. "He Wrote Our 'Tough-Love Santa Song.'" *Tampa Bay Times* (Florida), December 24, 1994, updated October 8, 2005.

Sheet Music Leaders chart. *Billboard*, December 29, 1934.

Suess, Jeff. "Our History: Covington Lyricist Penned Classic 'Santa Claus Is Comin' to Town.'" *Cincinnati Enquirer*, December 20, 2017.

John & Yoko and the Plastic Ono Band with the Harlem Community Choir, "Happy Xmas (War Is Over)"

The Beatles Bible. "John Lennon and Yoko Ono's 'War Is Over' Poster Campaign Is Launched." Accessed via www.beatlesbible.com.

Blaney, John. *John Lennon: Listen to This Book*. United Kingdom: Paper Jukebox, 2005.

Gilmore, Mikal. "Lennon Lives Forever." *Rolling Stone*, December 15, 2005. As published on dailykos.com.

Williams, Richard. "John Lennon: 'I Was Sick of White Christmas'—A Classic Interview from the Vaults." *Uncut*, 1998. As published in *Guardian* (London, England), December 13, 2011.

Joni Mitchell, "River"

Montagne, Renee. "The Music Midnight Makes: In Conversation with Joni Mitchell." NPR, December 9, 2014.

Recordings of "River." Accessed via jonimitchell.com.

Elton John, "Step into Christmas"

Daw, Stephen. "Ed Sheeran Reveals Upcoming Christmas Song with Elton John." *Billboard*, October 6, 2021.

"Diamond Moments: 'Step into Christmas.'"

December 14, 2017. Accessed via eltonjohn.com.

Slade, "Merry Xmas Everybody"

Hattenstone, Simon. "Christmas Hits: Are Slade, Boney M and the Pogues Made for Life?" *Guardian* (London, England), December 23, 2011.

Pelley, Rich. "'Everybody Wants to Know How Much I Make': Noddy Holder on Merry Xmas Everybody." *Guardian* (London, England), December 22, 2021.

Wizzard, "I Wish It Could Be Christmas Everyday"

Black, Johnny. "The Making of Wizzard's 'I Wish It Could Be Christmas Everyday'—A classic interview from the vaults." *Q*, 1996. As published in the *Guardian* (London, England), December 20, 2011.

Emmet Otter's Jug-Band Christmas, "Our World/Brothers"

Weinert-Kendt, Rob. "Paul Williams Rediscovers the Fun in 'Emmet Otter.'" *American Theatre*, December 7, 2021.

The Kinks, "Father Christmas"

Denselow, Robin. "Ray Davies of the Fashion-Defying Kinks." *Guardian* (London, England), December 23, 1977.

KindaKinks.net—Dave Emlen's Unofficial Kinks Web Site. "Father Christmas/Prince of the Punks." Accessed via kindakinks.net.

The Kinks Christmas Concert 1977. Accessed via youtube.com/watch?v=vRSCAoxOXVo.

"The Kinks' Dave Davies Says Band's Classic Holiday Song 'Father Christmas' Is 'Very Special to Me.'" ABC Audio, December 24, 2018.

Big Star, "Jesus Christ"

Beaugez, Jim. "Big Star's #1 Record Turns 50." *Garden and Gun*, October 27, 2022.

Dow, Mike. "Inside Big Star's 'Complete Third.'" *Maine Edge* (Bangor, Maine), November 23, 2016.

Eagles, "Please Come Home for Christmas"

Nager, Larry. "Charles Brown Recalls High-Rolling Newport Era." *Cincinnati Post*, August 18, 1990.

Rosen, Steven. "Christmas Song Has Mysterious Local Roots." *Cincinnati Enquirer*, December 18, 2014.

Kurtis Blow, "Christmas Rappin'"

Adler, Bill. "Every Year Just 'Bout This Time, Kurtis Blow Celebrates with a Rhyme." *Smithsonian*, December 3, 2019.

George, Nelson. *The Death of Rhythm & Blues*. New York: Penguin, 2003.

Lowers, Erin. "Kurtis Blow and Russell Simmons Tell the Story Behind 'Christmas Rappin'." *Hip-Hop Evolution*, December 19, 2016.

Quan, Jay. "Everything You Don't Know About Kurtis Blow's 'Christmas Rappin'." Accessed via rockthebells.com.

Ross, Alex Robert. "How an Early Christmas Single Helped Hip-Hop Explode." *Vice*, December 18, 2018.

Kate Bush, "December Will Be Magic Again"

Kate Bush Encyclopedia. "December Will Be Magic Again." Accessed via katebushencyclopedia.com.

Kate Bush News. "Abbey Road Studios Celebrate 'December Will Be Magic Again.'" December 21, 2020. Accessed via katebushnews.com.

John Denver and the Muppets, "When the River Meets the Sea"

Jim Henson's Red Book. "Air John Denver Christmas Special, San Diego Museum of Art, December 5, 1979." Accessed via henson.com/jimsredbook.

Elmo & Patsy, "Grandma Got Run Over by a Reindeer"

Associated Press. "Christmas with a Red-Nosed Grandma." *Akron Beacon Journal* (Akron, Ohio), December 13, 1979.

Cowan, Peter. "Elmo and Patsy Spin off Santa Claus." *Oakland Tribune* (Oakland, California), December 16, 1979.

Flick, David. "'Grandma' Still Kicks as Christmas Classic." *Dallas Morning News*, 1996.

UPI. "Runaway Reindeer Song Is Popular." *Chico Enterprise-Record* (Chico, California), December 29, 1979.

Paul McCartney, "Wonderful Christmastime"

Kinos-Goodin, Jesse. "Behind Paul McCartney's 'Wonderful Christmastime,' a Misunderstood Holiday Classic." CBC, December 21, 2017.

The Paul McCartney Project. "Wonderful Christmastime/Rudolph the Red-Nosed Reggae." Accessed via the-paulmccartney-project.com.

Sorcinelli, Gino. "Sampling and Replaying 'Wonderful Christmastime.'" December 21, 2020. Accessed via microchop.substack.com.

Billy Squier, "Christmas Is the Time to Say 'I Love You'"

"East Coastings." *Cash Box*, September 5, 1981.

Giles, Jeff. "How Billy Squier Ended Up Leading an On-Air MTV Holiday Singalong." *Ultimate Classic Rock*, December 18, 2017.

Parker, Lyndsey. "Martha, Martha, Martha! 35 Years Later, Original VJ Quinn Remembers MTV's Early Days." Yahoo!, August 1, 2016.

The Waitresses, "Christmas Wrapping"

Parker, Lyndsey. "Couldn't Miss This One This Year: The Surprisingly Complex Legacy of the Waitresses' 'Christmas Wrapping'." Yahoo!, December 21, 2021.

Price, Mark. "'Christmas Wrapping,' an Unlikely Hit for the Waitresses, Spreads Cheer 40 Years Later." *Akron Beacon Journal* (Akron, Ohio), December 5, 2021.

Simpson, Dave. "Christmas Wrapping: The Waitresses on How They Made a Festive Classic." *Guardian* (London, England), December 13, 2020.

David Bowie & Bing Crosby, "Peace on Earth/Little Drummer Boy"

Associated Press. "Bing Crosby's Kids Recall Dad's Surprise Duet with David Bowie." *Billboard*, July 24, 2014.

Farhi, Paul. "Bing and Bowie: An Odd Story of Holiday Harmony." *Washington Post*, December 19, 2006.

Dolly Parton, "Hard Candy Christmas"

Taggart, Patrick. "Making Dolly Happy." *Austin-*

American Statesman (Austin, Texas), February 28, 1982.

The Pretenders, "2000 Miles"

Buskin, Richard. "CLASSIC TRACKS: The Pretenders 'Back on the Chain Gang.'" *Sound on Sound*, September 2005.

"Hynde Sighted." *Record Mirror*, November 5, 1983.

Pretenders, "2000 Miles" and interview. *Countdown*, 1983. Accessed via youtube.com/watch?v=Q9l0sMNh3Sg.

Tyler, Kieron. "The Pretenders: Notes on 15 Singles." Sleeve notes, *Pirate Radio*, Rhino Records, March 2006.

Zimmer, Dave. "Spending Time with the Pretenders' Chrissie Hynde." *BAM*, August 24, 1984.

XTC (aka the Three Wise Men), "Thanks for Christmas"

Chalkhills: The XTC Resource. "Andy Discusses 'Thanks for Christmas.' Song of the Week—Andy's Take." Accessed via chalkhills.org/articles/XTCFans20061218.html.

Band Aid, "Do They Know It's Christmas?"

Clark-Meads, Jeff. "Band Aid Bonanza!" *Music Week*, December 15, 1984.

"On This Day in 1984: Band Aid Released 'Do They Know It's Christmas?'" *Hot Press*, December 3, 2020.

Mannheim Steamroller, "Deck the Halls"

Bahr, Jeff. "Omaha Group Rockets to No. 3 on Holiday Charts." *Lincoln Star* (Lincoln, Nebraska), December 27, 1984.

"An Interview with Chip Davis of Mannheim Steamroller Christmas." *New Jersey Stage*, December 4, 2018.

Ochs, Meredith. "How a Trucker's Protest Anthem Became a '70s Hit." NPR, June 6, 2017.

Prince, "Another Lonely Christmas"

Interview with Prince. Love4OneAnother.com, November 17, 1997.

Irwin, Corey. "How Prince Created 'Another Lonely Christmas.'" Ultimate Prince, December 24, 2019.

Prince Vault. "Another Lonely Christmas." Accessed via princevault.com.

Queen, "Thank God It's Christmas"

Interview with Brian May. *The Ultimate Classic Rock Nights* radio show, October 22, 2013.

Krol, Charlotte. "Queen Make Animated Video for 'Thank God It's Christmas' 35 Years After Festive Single Released." *NME*, December 16, 2019.

Kenny Rogers & Dolly Parton, "The Greatest Gift of All"

"Country Column / Ho, Ho, Ho." *Cashbox*, November 3, 1984.

Rogers, Kenny. Track comments from *Through the Years: A Retrospective* boxed set, 1998.

Wham!, "Last Christmas"

Aroesti, Rachel. "Still Saving Us from Tears: The Inside Story of Wham!'s Last Christmas." *Guardian* (London, England), December 14, 2017.

Eames, Tom. "The Story of . . . 'Last Christmas' by Wham!—as Told by Andrew Ridgeley." Smooth Radio, December 21, 2021.

Zaleski, Annie. "The Soulful Revenge of 'Last Christmas,' Wham!'s Potent Yuletide Breakup Song." Salon, December 25, 2021.

King Diamond, "No Presents for Christmas"

Christopher, Michael. "King Diamond on Rocking Corpse Paint, His 'Final Tour' and Why There Are No Presents for Christmas." Vanyaland, November 24, 2015.

"Weird Al" Yankovic, "Christmas at Ground Zero"

Adams, Erik. "'Weird Al' Yankovic Will Be Ham for the Holidays." *A.V. Club*, December 25, 2009.

Stingley, Mick. "'Weird Al' Talks About His 'Sick and Twisted' Music Parodies." *Esquire*, July 21, 2014.

Eurythmics, "Winter Wonderland"

Becker, Peter. "LOCAL HISTORY: Who Taught Music to Dick Smith?" *Tri-County Independent* (Honesdale, Pennsylvania), December 25, 2020.

Martin, Harry. "Footlights and Flickers." *Memphis Commercial Appeal* (Tennessee), November 29, 1934.

McNulty, Bernadette. "Annie Lennox: My Christmas Songs." *Telegraph* (UK), December 15, 2010.

Whitney Houston, "Do You Hear What I Hear?"

Brown, Jay. "Do You Hear What I Hear?': The Story Behind the Song." *St. Anthony Messenger*, December 2017.

"Do You Hear What I Hear?" Accessed via whitneyhouston.com.

"Harry Simeone Chorale, Do You Hear What I Hear—Review." *Billboard*, December 8, 1962.

Noland, Claire. "Gloria Shayne Baker: 1923–2008." *Chicago Tribune*, March 16, 2008.

John Cougar Mellencamp, "I Saw Mommy Kissing Santa Claus"

Adams, Magee. "Ban Urged on 'Mommy Kissing Santa.'" *Cincinnati Enquirer*, December 19, 1952.

Mabbott, Lucille. "Adventures in Music." *Rapid City Journal* (Rapid City, South Dakota), December 14, 1952.

The Pogues featuring Kirsty MacColl, "Fairytale of New York"

"Fairytale of New York: BBC Radio 1 Will Not Play Original Version." BBC, November 19, 2020.

Hodgkinson, Will. "Shane MacGowan: 'A Lot of Rock Stars Become Assholes.'" *Times* (UK), October 8, 2022.

Lynskey, Dorian. "Fairytale of New York: The Surprising Story Behind The Pogues' Christmas Anthem." *Irish Times* (Dublin, Ireland), December 7, 2020.

Run-DMC, "Christmas in Hollis"

Rytlewski, Evan. "We Talk Run-DMC's 'Christmas in Hollis' with DMC Himself." *A.V. Club*, December 10, 2013.

Bruce Springsteen, "Merry Christmas Baby"

Browning, William. "Who Really Wrote 'Merry Christmas, Baby.'" *Smithsonian*, November 2017.

Brucebase. "Merry Christmas Baby." Accessed via brucebase.wikidot.com.

Charles Brown performs "Merry Christmas Baby" at Jazz Fest 1990 (Video). Accessed via facebook.com.

Al Green & Annie Lennox, "Put a Little Love in Your Heart"

McDonough, Jimmy. *Soul Survivor: A Biography of Al Green*. Boston, Massachusetts: Da Capo Press, 2017. Al Green interview quoted in *Birmingham Post-Herald* (Birmingham, Alabama), May 18, 1982.

Pollock, Bruce. "Jackie DeShannon, 'Put a Little Love in Your Heart.'" SongFacts, December 11, 2012.

Chris Rea, "Driving Home for Christmas"

The One Show. "How Chris Rea Wrote 'Driving Home for Christmas.'" Accessed via youtube.com/watch?v=LrdW5iP9xZo.

Rea, Chris. "Chris Rea on 'Driving Home for Christmas' | The Story Behind." Accessed via youtube.com/watch?v=fwLt_nR3KjQ.

Simpson, Dave. "Chris Rea: How We Made Driving Home for Christmas." *Guardian* (London, England), December 19, 2016.

Ramones, "Merry Christmas (I Don't Want to Fight Tonight)"

"Video Track." *Billboard*, December 23, 1989.

AC/DC, "Mistress for Christmas"

Angus Young interview. *Guitar World*, February 1991.

Tom Petty & the Heartbreakers, "Christmas All Over Again"

Interview with Tom Petty. Liner notes, Tom Petty and the Heartbreakers, *Playback* boxed set, 1995.

"Tom Petty Behind the Scenes: 'It's Christmas All Over Again'" (Video). Accessed via youtube.com/watch?v=qUq2sZpuDPM.

TLC, "Sleigh Ride"

Ross, Alex Robert. "25 Whole Years Ago, TLC Finally Made Christmas Sound Fun on 'Sleigh Ride.'" *Vice*, December 4, 2018.

Mariah Carey, "All I Want for Christmas Is You"

Coscarelli, Joe. "How Mariah Carey's 'All I Want for Christmas Is You' Finally Hit No. 1." *New York Times*, December 20, 2019.

Dresdale, Andrea. "'It Makes Me Happy': Mariah Carey Reveals What 'All I Want for Christmas Is You' Means to Her Now." ABC Radio, December 7, 2020.

McIntyre, Hugh. "Mariah Carey's 'All I Want for Christmas Is You' Becomes the First Holiday Single to Be Certified Diamond." *Forbes*, December 3, 2021.

Rosen, Craig. "Mariah Carey Wraps Up Xmas Album." *Billboard*, October 8, 1994.

Ryan, Patrick. "Mariah Carey on 'All I Want for Christmas Is You' Turning 25: 'I Don't Acknowledge Time.'" *USA Today*, November 1, 2019.

Trust, Gary. "Wish Come True: Mariah Carey's 'All I Want for Christmas Is You' Hits No. 1 on Hot 100 After 25-Year Wait." *Billboard*, December 16, 2019.

The Vandals, "Oi to the World!"

Hefflon, Scott. "An Interview with Guitarist Warren Fitzgerald." *Lollipop* magazine, September 1, 2000.

Mugabe, Boz. Interview with Joe Escalante and Warren Fitzgerald of the Vandals. *Nosebleed*, February 1999. Accessed via scatalogik.com.

Trans-Siberian Orchestra, "Christmas Eve/Sarajevo 12/24"

Billboard staff. "What Are the Top-Selling Holiday Songs?" *Billboard*, November 25, 2016.

Breimeier, Russ. "A Christmas Story." *Christianity Today*, December 22, 2003.

Fountains of Wayne, "I Want an Alien for Christmas"
Out-of-State Plates liner notes, 2005.

NSYNC, "Merry Christmas, Happy Holidays"

LeBlanc, Larry. "Vince Degiorgio—Songwriter and Publisher Profile." Accessed via itallstartswithasong.wordpress.com.

Destiny's Child, "8 Days of Christmas"

Van Horn, Teri. "Destiny's Child Put 'Stank' into Christmas on Holiday Album." MTV News, September 24, 2001.

Barenaked Ladies & Sarah McLachlan, "God Rest Ye Merry Gentlemen"

Lyrics, "Sit You Merry Gentlemen." Accessed via csufresno.edu/folklore/Olson.

Monthly Review. vol. 31, 1764. Accessed via babel.hathitrust.org.

Sandys, W. B. *Christmas Carols, Ancient and Modern*. London: Richard Beckley, 1833.

Schonberg, Harold C. "God Rest You, Wandering Comma." *The New York Times*, December 26, 1971.

Sheet verse. "Three New Christmas Carols." 1760. Accessed via searchworks.stanford.edu.

Zaleski, Annie. "Before the O.C. Celebrated Chrismukkah, Maybe This Christmas Spread Hip Holiday Cheer." *A.V. Club*, December 15, 2014.

Josh Groban, "O Holy Night"

Edwards, David. "O Holy Night." *Ukiah Daily Journal* (Ukiah, California), December 24, 2004.

The Hymns and Carols of Christmas. "*Cantique de Noël*." Accessed via hymnsandcarolsofchristmas.com.

Joop's Musical Flowers. "Cantique de Noël/ Minuit Chretien (1847) / O Holy Night (1855) / O Helga Natt (1899) / Kerstnacht (1921)." December 28, 2016. Accessed via jopiepopie.blogspot.com.

"Reminder: 'O Holy Night' Started Out as an Abolitionist Anthem." Relevant, December 8, 2020.

White Stripes, "Candy Cane Children"

News, White Stripes, 2002. Accessed via whitestripes.com.

Urban Dictionary. "Candy Cane Children." Accessed via urbandictionary.com.

The Darkness, "Christmas Time (Don't Let the Bells End)"

Kielty, Martin. "Justin Hawkins Wishes the Darkness Didn't Write Christmas Song." *Ultimate Classic Rock*, February 7, 2022.

May, Rebecca. "Exclusive Interview: The Darkness' Justin Hawkins Reveals His 5 Favourite Christmas Songs." *ShortList*, December 14, 2019.

Whitney Houston, "The First Noel"

The Hymns and Carols of Christmas. "Christmas Carols Ancient and Modern—William Sandys." Accessed via hymnsandcarolsofchristmas.com.

Online Etymology Dictionary. "Noel (n.)." Accessed via etymonline.com.

The Killers, "A Great Big Sled"

Adams, Guy. "The Killers: Why We're Having a RED Christmas." *Independent* (UK), December 1, 2006.

The Global Fund. "15 Years of Red." January 26, 2021. Accessed via theglobalfund.org.

Montgomery, James. "Killers Help Out Bono by 'Representin' the North Pole.'" MTV News, November 30, 2006.

SongFacts. "The Killers, 'A Great Big Sled.'" Accessed via SongFacts.

Lady Gaga, "Christmas Tree"

Vazquez, Michael. "A Space Cowboy Odyssey (Video)." *Urb*, December 10, 2009.

Bob Dylan, "Must Be Santa"

Flanagan, Bill. "Exclusive Bob Dylan Interview." International Network of Street Papers, November 23, 2009.

Justin Bieber, "Mistletoe"

Caulfield, Keith. "Justin Bieber's 'Mistletoe' Brightens Billboard 200 with No. 1 Debut." *Billboard*, November 9, 2011.

Vena, Jocelyn. "Justin Bieber Gets Romantic in 'Mistletoe' Teaser." MTV News, October 11, 2011.

Michael Bublé,
"It's Beginning to Look a Lot Like Christmas"

Medel, Brian. "Christmas Looks a Lot like Yarmouth in Classic Tune." *Chronicle Herald* (Yarmouth, Nova Scotia, Canada), November 20, 2011.

Warner Records. "Michael Bublé Christmas 2021 Super Deluxe 10th Anniversary Limited Edition Box Set" (Press Release), September 17, 2021. Accessed via prnewswire.com.

Kelly Clarkson, "Underneath the Tree"

"Kelly Clarkson, Ariana Grande and Justin Bieber Top ASCAP New Classic Holiday Songs Chart" (Press Release), December 9, 2021. Accessed via www.ascap.com.

Ariana Grande, "Santa Tell Me"

"Kelly Clarkson, Ariana Grande and Justin Bieber Top ASCAP New Classic Holiday Songs Chart" (Press Release), December 9, 2021. Accessed via www.ascap.com.

Pentatonix, "Carol of the Bells"

Carnegie Hall schedule, Ukrainian National Chorus, October 5, 2022.

Rice University News Staff. "'Carol of the Bells' Wasn't Originally a Christmas Song," December 13, 2004. eurekalert.org.

Tomkiw, Lydia. "Toll of the Bells." *Slate*, December 19, 2019.

Andra Day & Stevie Wonder,
"Someday at Christmas"

"Andra Day Talks About Working with Stevie Wonder & Music Influences" (Video). Live 101.5 Phoenix. Accessed via youtube.com/watch?v=fi3pbwJmSm8.

"Stevie Wonder: Someday at Christmas" (Album Review). *Billboard*, December 23, 1967.

"Wonder Duets." Accessed via steviewonder.org.uk.

Taylor Swift, "Christmas Tree Farm"

Fox, Courtney. "Taylor Swift Grew Up on a Christmas Tree Farm in Pennsylvania." *Wide Open Country*, December 11, 2021.

Grigoriadis, Vanessa. "The Very Pink, Very Perfect Life of Taylor Swift." *Rolling Stone*, March 5, 2009.

Moser, John J. "Taylor Swift Reconnects with Pennsylvania Roots: Talks about Playing Croc Rock, Visits Childhood Home in Berks." *Morning Call* (Allentown, Pennsylvania), July 16, 2018.

"Taylor Swift: The Making of Christmas Tree Farm" (Video). Taylor Swift—official YouTube channel. Accessed via youtube.com/watch?v=O2Irnn7F1PM.

"Taylor Swift on Her Old Timey Version of Christmas Tree Farm" (Video). Amazon Music. Accessed via youtube.com/watch?v=BE3oAPFHYfc.

Index

About the Author

Annie Zaleski is an author, editor, and journalist with a focus on music and pop culture. Her work has appeared in dozens of publications, including *NPR Music*, the *Guardian*, *Time*, *Rolling Stone*, *Salon*, *Billboard*, the *A.V. Club*, *Vulture*, *Alternative Press*, *Stereogum*, the *Village Voice*, *The Los Angeles Times*, and the *Cleveland Plain Dealer*. She is the author of a 33 1/3 book on Duran Duran's *Rio*, *Lady Gaga: Applause*, and *Pink: Raise Your Glass*, and contributed an essay to *Go All the Way: A Literary Appreciation of Power Pop*, among others. She lives in Cleveland, Ohio.